Embryos and Ethics

Embryos and Ethics
The Warnock Report in Debate

edited by

Nigel M. de S. Cameron
Warden of Rutherford House, Edinburgh

RUTHERFORD HOUSE BOOKS
Edinburgh

*Published by Rutherford House,
17 Claremont Park, Edinburgh EH6 7PJ, Scotland*

ISBN 0 946068 21 6 (casebound)
ISBN 0 946068 22 4 (limp)

Copyright © 1987 Rutherford House and Contributors

All rights reserved. No part of this publication may be reproduced, stored in a retrieval system, or transmitted, in any form, by any means, electronic, mechanical, photocopying, recording or otherwise without the prior permission of Rutherford House.

Computer typeset at Rutherford House on Apple Macintosh Plus.
Printed by Chong Moh, Singapore.

In Memory of Ian Donald, CBE
1910 - 1987

CONTENTS

Preface   ix

Foreword   xi
Sir John Peel, KCVO

1. **The Christian Stake in the Warnock Debate**   1
   The Revd Dr Nigel M. de S. Cameron

2. **In Vitro Fertilisation: the Major Issues**   14
   Dr Teresa Iglesias

3. **The Ethics of Experimentation**   28
   Dr Richard Higginson

4. **Some Theological Perspectives on the Human Embryo**   43
   The Revd Dr David Atkinson

5. **What Kind of Being is the Human Embryo?**   58
   Dr Teresa Iglesias

6. **Problems Raised by Artificial Human Reproduction**   74
   The late Professor Ian Donald

7. **Responses to Warnock: a Review**   82
   Dr Isobel K. Grigor

8. **After the Embryo the Fetus?**   91
   Sir John Peel

9. **Childless Couples and Rootless Children**   102
   Dr Richard Higginson

10. **A View from the Other End**   108
    Dr George L. Chalmers

Index   121

CONTRIBUTORS

The Revd Dr Nigel M. de S. Cameron is Warden of Rutherford House, Edinburgh.
Sir John Peel, KCVO is a Past President of the Royal College of Obstetricians and Gynaecologists.
Dr Teresa Iglesias is Lecturer in Ethics at University College, Dublin.
Dr Richard Higginson is Tutor in Ethics at Cranmer Hall Durham.
The Revd Dr David Atkinson is Chaplain of Corpus Christi College, Oxford.
The late Professor Ian Donald, CBE, was Regius Professor of Midwifery, University of Glasgow.
Dr Isobel K. Grigor is Social Interests Secretary of the Board of Social Responsibility, Church of Scotland.
Dr George L. Chalmers is Consultant in Administrative Charge, Glasgow East District Geriatric Service.

ACKNOWLEDGEMENTS

Some of the material in chapter 1 was included in Dr Cameron's Biblical Creation Lecture for 1986.
Chapter 2 was first published in the *Journal of Medical Ethics*, 1984, vol. 1, pp. 32 - 37, and is used by permission.
Chapters 4,5,6,7,8, and 10 were first published in *Ethics and Medicine*: chapters 4 and 5 in 2.1, chapter 6 in 1.2, chapters 7 and 8 in 2.2 and chapter 10 in 1.2.
The material in chapter 9 also appears in Dr Higginson's Grove Booklet on the Warnock Report, 1986.

PREFACE

There can be no doubt that the cluster of questions associated with *in vitro* fertilisation and the treatment of the human embryo are among the gravest which will be faced by this generation. The revolution in reproductive technology has provided the human race with an unparallelled opportunity to manipulate our own kind, by intervention in the process of generation itself, and by the use of the early human subject for purposes of experiment. Since Britain has played a leading role in the development of IVF, the outcome of our ethical and legal discussions is awaited with particular interest in other countries where these matters are under review.

This volume brings together essays in philosophy and theology with contributions from distinguished clinicians. Their writers share a common concern for the human values of the Judaeo-Christian tradition which have been so influential in shaping the pattern of western medical practice. They believe that these values are threatened at a fundamental level by this technology and the use to which it is being put. Their response to the Warnock Report and the settlement which it advocates is one of sadness at Warnock's failure to grapple with the profoundly important ethical issues at stake, allied with deep anxiety as to what the future may hold.

Most of the volume was already in type when we had news of the death of one of our contributors, Professor Ian Donald, CBE. It is fitting that we should dedicate this book to his memory.

Nigel M. de S. Cameron
Rutherford House,
Edinburgh
July 23rd, 1987

FOREWORD

Sir John Peel

In writing a brief foreword to this symposium, I am conscious of the enormous importance of the subject. When Louise Brown was born a few years ago, a child conceived as the result of the fertilisation of her mother's egg by her father's sperm *in vitro* in the laboratory, the general public as well as the medical professions hailed it as a scientific medical triumph. With thought focused on the plight of the infertile couple, little thought was given to the potential dangers that might result, any more than thoughts of the atomic bomb penetrated people's minds when the atom was first split.

Progress has been frighteningly rapid since Louise Brown, bringing in its train a veritable explosion of problems - scientific, medical, social, ethical, legal and economic. The fact that the Warnock Committee, set up to examine these problems, failed to produce a unanimous report emphasises the immensity of the problems and the fact that the debate is by no means over.

The pages that follow, written by eminent men and women in their own spheres, give an authoritative account of the facts that society must face. In this, as in some other spheres of modern technological progress in medicine, one cannot help wondering just how much of a contribution is being made to the ultimate happiness of the human race. *In vitro* fertilisation is not, of course, a cure for infertility but a device for 'assisting' an infertile woman - any woman, regardless of her state - to have a child. Is the primacy to be accorded to the wishes of the woman or to the ultimate well-being of the child? They will not always coincide.

But much more fundamental is the question of where science, left to its own devices, will take us in relation to reproduction in the human race. Science has driven on relentlessly, and always will, in its quest for new fields to conquer. With banks of human sperms and human eggs frozen and stored in various laboratories throughout the world, available for putting together to form embryos, fetuses and children, are there no pitfalls for society to fall into? We have been warned. Do we want veterinary type selective breeding in human reproduction, already suggested as a possibility? Do we want human beings conceived in the laboratory, and reared and nourished there with the aid of an artificial placenta? These are not mere fantasies but real possibilities if science is given a totally free hand. Are we not pandering to what the Greeks called *hubris* - the overweening pride, in this case of the scientist; and may there not follow the inevitable *nemesis*?

These are profound questions to which all society must turn its most serious attention. What follows will, I hope, help those who read this book to face the facts and reach a mature judgement.

THE CHRISTIAN STAKE IN THE WARNOCK DEBATE

NIGEL M. DE S. CAMERON

When Mrs Mary Warnock, as she then was, accepted the invitation of Her Majesty's Government in July of 1982 to chair a Committee of Inquiry into the 'social, ethical and legal implications of recent, and potential developments in the field of human assisted reproduction',[1] she can hardly have realised what lay in store. Already the veteran of one respected inquiry report, Mrs (now Baroness) Warnock combined experience in education with the reputation of a distinguished moral philosopher. There was comfort in some circles that the Committee was chaired by someone from outside the medical profession. Indeed, the fact that she was not only a moral philosopher but one with the common touch (such that her reputation reached readers of women's magazines as well as the Senior Common Rooms of Oxbridge) was seen to augur well. The moral issues, to be sure, were not the only issues to be examined. But, it was presumed, they would be given pride of place. Would they not?

So, while controversy was expected, the furore which greeted the publication of the report could not have been anticipated. And yet its intensity would be hard to exaggerate. In the first airing of views in Parliament the tone of debates in both Commons and Lords was decidedly hostile to the settlement advocated in the report. As a result, Private Members' legislation was introduced into the House of Commons in an attempt to overturn its chief recommendation, legislation which on its introduction received overwhelming Parliamentary approval. The House of Commons became the scene of unprecedented procedural manoeuvres, both by its supporters and also by those who sought to interdict its passage into law. And in support of the *Unborn Children (Protection) Bill*, introduced by the Right Honourable Enoch Powell, M.P., the House was presented

---

1. *Report of the Committee of Inquiry into Human Fertilisation and Embryology*, Cmnd. 9314, London, 1984, p. iv.

with the largest public petition since the Chartists.

In the event, by means of procedural devices, the Bill's passage was successfully prevented; but the support which it received would seem to have foreclosed any Government hopes of legislating in line with the recommendations of the Warnock Committee. Since there is no existing framework of law governing most of the practices on which Warnock reported, the result of this stalemate has been that in many areas, including that of embryo research, the only constraints are those of technique - together with some voluntary agreement which has been reached by medical scientists along Warnock lines. As this volume goes to press (in the spring of 1987) the Government has invited further comments on the issues raised in the Warnock Report with a view to introducing legislation at an early opportunity, permitting a free vote between alternative clauses on the central question of the employment of the human embryo for purposes of deleterious research.

Why the furore? The majority on the Warnock Committee sought a settlement of crucial disputed issues by means of compromise. The sole exception was the question of surrogacy, on which an uncharacteristically firm position was taken up. On the central matter of the use of human embryos for the purposes of deleterious research, the majority recommendation was that this should be permitted up to the age of fourteen days. While in one sense this could be seen as a compromise position (since higher figures had been canvassed, and were preferred by some of those working in the field), it was at the same time no compromise at all, since it conceded the principle at the heart of the entire debate, that a human embryo may be regarded as a fit subject of vivisection. To those who find this idea to be not merely wrong, but incomprehensibly evil, the question whether it should continue for ten days or fourteen or seventeen is, at best, of secondary significance. It is no surprise that this issue, which roused such public and political passions, attracted two of Warnock's three Expressions of Dissent. Since they have not been widely reported it is worth noting them before we go further.

Dissent B argued against any use of human embryos for purposes of research, and was signed by three members. They called for the protection of the human embryo in law. Although, they maintained, 'it is right that efforts should be made to alleviate' infertility, and although 'the advance of scientific knowledge is likewise of great value', neither of these ends justifies the 'deliberate destruction' of human embryos.[2] The four signatories of Dissent C were prepared to accept the experimental use of 'spare' embryos, that is, embryos whose existence had come about as a by-product of *in vitro* fertilisation undertaken with a view to enabling a woman to become pregnant. But they too rejected the deliberate creation of embryos for experimental purposes. This is of considerable interest, and it is surprising that it has gone largely unremarked since, between them, these two Dissents drew support from a total of seven members of the committee, that is to say, from just one less than half its complement. Had only one other member chosen to oppose it, the principal recommendation of the Warnock Committee, that 'research should be permitted on embryos brought into existence specifically for that purpose or coming into existence as a result of other research',[3] could never have been framed as a majority recommendation at all. This in itself indicates the weight which must be attached to the widespread public and political rejection of the settlement advocated in the name of Warnock.[4]

The essays collected in this volume address central questions discussed in the report from a number of different vantage-points. The method of approach is partly topical, partly disci-

---

2. *Ibid.*, pp. 90-93.
3. *Ibid.*, p. 69.
4. It needs also to be remembered that persons of pronounced opinion are not generally put on committees of inquiry, which are designed to provide compromises. None of the distinguished moral philososophers or churchmen who had publicly taken up conservative positions on the ethical issues under discussion was invited to serve on Warnock. Even the more conservative of the Dissents was argued on the ground of the 'potential', rather than 'actual' personhood of the embryo.

   It is interesting to note that although it was claimed that the membership of the committee 'encompassed not only the many professions with a concern in these matters but the many religious traditions within society, so that as many viewpoints as possible could be brought to bear on the sensitive issues before us,' *ibid.*, p. iv, the choice was not made by religious bodies themselves; so while the

plinary. Inevitably in a composite work of this kind, in which the same issues are brought into focus from different angles, there is some degree of overlap in treatment. No attempt has been made to excise it, and it will be of interest and benefit to the reader to discover how different minds arrive at similar conclusions by different paths.

The nub of the case against Warnock can be simply put. The central question at issue is that of the treatment of the human embryo - not simply in research, but in freezing, giving, buying and selling, and destruction. Behind this practical question lies another, the question of the *nature* of the human embryo. We can never know how to treat something before we know what, or who, it is. And yet the Warnock Report avoids asking, and therefore attempting to answer, that question. Its authors do not even get round to discussing it until they have already spent ten chapters examining techniques for the relief of infertility. When, finally, they do, it is in the context of a chapter entitled 'Scientific Issues'. The committee write:

> Although the questions of when life or personhood begin appear to be susceptible of straightforward answers, we hold that the answers to such questions in fact are complex amalgams of factual and moral judgements. Instead of trying to answer these questions directly we have therefore gone straight to the question of *how it is right to treat the human embryo.*[5]

That is, they have deliberately chosen not to address the single question on which all of the other, lesser, questions depend. Moreover, the manner in which the question of the nature of the embryo is dismissed is itself deceptive. It implies that those who hold that the question is susceptible of an answer implicitly deny that 'complex amalgams of factual and moral judgements' may be necessary in order to arrive at it. In other words, their approach to the subject lacks the sophistication which an adequate assessment requires. Yet, of course, it is entirely possible to

---

committee included at least one member of each of several such, their appointments, like the opinions of some of them, lacked any representative character.

5. *Ibid.*, p. 60. Italics original.

come to a 'straightforward' answer by means of a complex argument, and Warnock received evidence from some distinguished persons who did just that.[6]

If it is true, as several of the essays which follow argue, that the only way in which we can make sense of the human embryo is to regard it for moral purposes as the human being the biologist has already found it to be, the question of embryo research is the ultimate question man faces as he considers his relations with his fellows. That is, the question of embryo research ceases to be a distinct question. It becomes rather an example of a general question, the old question of the propriety of the experimental use of human subjects. The human embryo ceases to be 'human material' deserving of some special category of respect, and becomes instead 'one of us', a human existence, the life of a fellow-member of our own species. The morality of embryo research is therefore the morality of all human research. And there has long been a consensus that involuntary research that may harm and cannot benefit its human subject is ethically indefensible.

One of the major contributors to international debate on what we are coming to know as 'Warnock issues' is Peter Singer, of the Department of Philosophy in Monash University in Australia. The Queen Victoria Medical Centre in Melbourne, connected with the University, has made many headlines for its pioneering work in the field of reproductive technology, and a number of important publications have issued from biologists, philosophers and others associated with Monash. Furthermore, 1987 saw the foundation of a new international journal entitled

---

6. For example, the Society for the Protection of Unborn Children invited, among others, Professor Paul Ramsey of Princeton University to submit evidence on its behalf. His essay, 'The Issues Facing Mankind', was published by the Society in *The Question of In Vitro Fertilization: Studies in Medicine, Law and Ethics* and reprinted in *Ethics and Medicine* 1:3 (1985). Indeed, the fact that an argument can be simply put says nothing about the sophistication with which it can also be put. Some of the more demanding essays in this volume are examples of this fact, as is Professor Oliver O'Donovan's difficult but very important book, *Begotten or Made?* Oxford, 1984.

Bioethics, under the joint editorship of Singer and his colleague Helga Kuhse.

Singer, who has (interestingly) written on animal liberation as well as the ethics of embryo research, has coined a new term, which serves to focus our thinking in this area with some clarity. He uses it in response to arguments against abortion and embryo research which assert that the embryo is a human being and therefore to be respected like all human beings. Writing with Helga Kuhse in the recent Monash symposium *Test-Tube Babies* he remarks:

> When opponents of abortion say that the embryo is a living human being from conception onwards, all they can possibly mean is that the embryo is a living member of the species *Homo sapiens*. That is all that can be established as a scientific fact. But is this also the sense in which every 'human being' has a right to life? We think not. To claim that every human being has a right to life solely because it is biologically a member of the species *Homo sapiens* is to make species membership the basis of rights. This is as indefensible as making race membership the basis of rights. It is the form of prejudice one of us has elsewhere referred to as 'speciesism', a prejudice in favour of members of one's own species, simply because they are members of one's own species. The logic of this prejudice runs parallel to the logic of the racist who is prejudiced in favour of members of his race simply because they are members of his race.

And he continues:

If we are to attribute rights on morally defensible grounds, we must base them on some morally relevant characteristic of the beings to whom we attribute rights. Examples of such morally relevant characteristics would be consciousness, autonomy, rationality, and so on, but not race or species.

Hence, although it may be possible to claim with strict literal accuracy that a human life exists from conception, it is not possible to claim that a human life exists from conception in the sense of a being which possesses, even at the most minimal level, the capacities distinctive of most human beings. Yet it is on the possession of these capacities that the attribution of a right to life, or of any other special moral status, must be based.[7]

A number of comments could be made on these statements. For one thing, it is interesting to note that they consist largely of assertions, rather than arguments. Secondly, Singer and Kuhse are forced by their candour to concede that the embryo is indeed a human being, and then to engage in sophistry in an attempt to avoid the implications of this admission. Thirdly, in their coinage of the concept of 'speciesism', they bring us directly to one of the chief issues at stake in this debate for the Christian. Let us take up these last two points in reverse order.

The charge of 'speciesism' is essentially a denial of crucial aspects of the Christian doctrine of the creation of man. Singer and Kuhse's approach to moral reasoning takes us a further stage away from the dignity of man as the ground of his rights. In place of his dignity *as man* we have his abilities, or lack of them, as 'morally relevant characteristics', in the writers' vocabulary.

But we should not conclude that this kind of defence of embryo experimentation is limited to people like Singer and Kuhse. Their contribution has been to flush out the essential presupposition of their argument, and we are right to consider it to be deeply embedded in an evolutionary world-view. The specialness of every individual man must be justified, since as a member of the species he is an animal like any other. So the fact that the human embryo is a member of *Homo sapiens* is not simply irrelevant if introduced into this discussion, it is worse (since speciesism is immoral). By contrast, what *is* relevant is to point out, as Singer and Kuhse do on the next page of their essay, that the early embryo is 'far inferior to a tadpole in respect of all characteristics that could be regarded as morally relevant'.

We can now turn back to our second remark, noting that Singer and Kuhse are able to make the candid admission that the embryo is a human being since they feel free to deny any general

---

7. Helga Kuhse and Peter Singer, 'The Moral Status of the Embryo', in *Test-Tube Babies*, ed. William Walters and Peter Singer, Melbourne, 1984, p. 60.

concept of human nature entailing human dignity and human rights. The assessment of 'morally relevant characteristics' is the only way in which moral worth may be determined. Not only is it admitted that human life begins at conception, but Singer and Kuhse go so far as to accept that it can be established as a 'scientific fact' that 'the embryo is a living member of the species *Homo sapiens*'.

Of course, this may seem little enough. How could it be denied, that the fusion of sperm and ovum in this species, as in every other, brings into being the offspring of the parents? Yet it takes us directly into the subject of the nature of the embryo with a candour which Warnock studiously managed to avoid. Singer and Kuhse seek a way out of their admission by rather glibly positing 'two possible senses of the term "human being"', but in seeking this way out they reveal the weakness of their position.

The Question of Potentiality

Before we go further it is as well to comment on the confused and confusing use of the idea of 'potential' as qualifying the human life of the embryo. No-one would wish to deny that there is much that is potential in the embryo, as, of course, there is also much that is potential in the new-born child. Indeed, there are many parallels between the two, for while certain features which are characteristic of human life are attained during the infant's development *in utero*, others do not appear until the first months, or indeed years, of the child's life; and it is only after adolescence that it makes sense to speak of the human being as having fully developed into what he or she was intended to become. Even then the story is by no means told.

What, then, is the relevance of talk of potentiality in the embryo? Does this category succeed in seriously qualifying the conclusions which we might wish to draw from the fact that the embryo is already a 'human being'? Singer and Kuhse certainly think so, and it is worth our continuing with their presentation for a little longer.

Having spoken of the inferiority of the embryo to the tadpole as a possessor of 'morally relevant characteristics', they ask, 'what of its potential? Unlike a tadpole', they continue, perceptively, 'it has the potential to develop into a normal human being, with a high degree of rationality, self-consciousness, autonomy, and so on. Can this potential justify the belief that the embryo is entitled to a special moral status?'

In denying the moral significance of the embryo's potential Singer and Kuhse adopt a parallel which has been commonly taken up in this discussion. They write as follows, employing an argument which is patently false:

> Everything that can be said about the potential of the embryo can also be said about the potential of the egg and the sperm. The egg and the sperm, if united, also have the potential to develop into a normal human being . . . . On the basis of our premise that the egg and the sperm separately have no special moral status, it seems impossible to use the potential of the embryo as a ground for giving it special moral status.[8]

It is no doubt true that a sperm and an egg are 'potentially' a human being (by which Singer and Kuhse seem to mean a born or perhaps adult human person - a 'human being' in their second, and morally relevant, sense), and it is also true that an embryo is 'potentially' that too. But the idea of 'potential' which is employed in these two cases is very different indeed. In one case (the separate sperm and egg) what we have is potentially something else altogether; in the other it is potentially merely the progression of its self. This point has been made with great clarity by Thomas F. Torrance, who must rank as one of the world's leading thinkers on the interface of scientific and religious thought and whose comment on the Warnock Report was that it gave him a 'fierce jolt' and 'outraged' his conscience 'at a deeper level than almost anything else' he had read in recent years.

Torrance, in his useful pamphlet entitled *Test-Tube Babies*, argues that

> If . . . we want to think of the human embryo as 'potentially person', that must be taken to mean, not that the embryo is in the process of becoming something else, but rather that the embryo continues to become what he or she already is . . . .[9]

---

8. *Ibid.*, p. 61.
9. Thomas F. Torrance, *Test-Tube Babies*, Edinburgh, 1984, p. 11.

That is to say, whereas sperm and ovum must become something else if they are to develop into an adult human being, the fertilised embryo must simply become itself, fulfilling the destiny which in its own nature it has already come to possess.

The Image of God

With this consideration of what the embryo is in itself, we are brought to the question of what it is in relation to God. Granted that the biological evidence would lead us to conclude that the human embryo, like every embryo, is a tiny but complete member of the species of its parents, do we have a distinct moral construction to place on this conclusion? Singer and Kuhse's dismissal of it stems from their concept of what matters about man, where man's moral significance lies, what (to use their terms) are morally *relevant* characteristics. For them, membership of the species is not relevant; worse, claims that it is are sheer prejudice.

The Biblical doctrine of man sets Singer's 'speciesism' nearly upon its head - nearly, because Scripture agrees that man is not to be absolutised. It is not *merely* because a man is a member of this species, let alone of *my* species, that I must afford him special rights and dignities. The ground of man's dignity lies neither in his being *Homo sapiens* nor in his being of the same species as me. Rather, it is because his particular form of being (man rather than gorilla, man rather than tadpole, man rather than tree) reflects and derives from God in a way in which none other does, that every man demands respect, from me and from every other creature.

With these qualifications, the Christian's rejection of Singer's attempted morality must be complete. The *imago Dei* with its reflection of and derivation from God is irrevocably bound to mankind. It is, as has been said, *species-specific*. It is difficult to see how any other exegesis of Genesis is possible, since Genesis 1, whatever else it is, provides a taxonomy of the created order. However we construe the scope of its biological categories, it is evident that the category 'man' is intended to be coterminous with what *we* mean by man. It refers to *Homo sapiens* as such, and is not concerned to distinguish between some members of the species and others, whether on the basis of race, religion, age, moral character, the presence and absence of particular qualities (rationality, the ability to communicate, or any of the possibilities which Singer and Kuhse choose to regard as 'morally relevant'), or anything else. What is made in the image of God is *man*, nothing more, nothing less.

We now take this argument a stage further.

The Incarnation

Alongside the general argument from the *imago Dei* there stands a specific argument from the case of Jesus Christ. The Bible contains many accounts of ante-natal life, particularly in the Old Testament, where many writers reflect on their life before birth. Some of these references are more valuable than others. In some contexts the chief interest of the writer is in the divine foreknowledge. If the reference goes back before conception, as some do, it is more difficult to regard it as relevant to the ontology of the product of conception, since there can be no question of its pre-existence. But some of the texts are of more help.

Yet in each case it has been suggested that the fact that a writer reflects on his origins in the womb need not have ontological implications for every intra-uterine life. For example, it might be necessary for an embryo or fetus to pass a certain point before gaining a status which would bear retrospective implications. So embryos dying *in vitro*, or even fetuses succumbing to abortion, would remain as possible persons rather than actual; while you and I and Jeremiah, having been actualised (at 14 days, 3 months, 6 months, birth, or whenever) are able to look back at the early origins of ourselves before this time and still say that 'that was I'.

This argument has a certain force, although not enough to do the job for which it has been constructed - to deflect the entire momentum of the Biblical witness to the character of intra-uterine life. Leaving to one side objections to the argument on its merits, it does not adequately meet the difficulties posed by some of the Biblical texts (which bear their own ontological implications). But it has no relevance to the most important of them all.

We may hesitate to suggest that the argument from the incarnation has a knock-down significance in this debate, but many will feel this to be the case.[10] It provides a theological argument of an altogether different kind to those which have traditionally been drawn from the Biblical text in controversy about abortion, for it depends not upon the interpretation of a particular statement, but on the most distinctive of all Christian doctrines.

According to the creed, the life-story of Jesus Christ upon earth began when he was conceived by the Virgin Mary through the miraculous agency of the Holy Spirit. In asserting this the creed follows the Gospel testimony, in which Mary is told that she will conceive as a result of the Holy Spirit 'coming upon' her, and being 'overshadowed' with the 'power of the Most High'. That is to say, the doctrine of the incarnation of Jesus Christ accords with the common-sense reading of the biological evidence that the act of incarnation took place not in Bethlehem where the baby was born, but before ever the journey to Bethlehem began. God became incarnate in an embryo, in the supernatural fertilisation of an ovum. There are several particular exegetical reasons for such a reading of the Lucan narrative, but even if the text were silent in the matter it would remain logically necessary to identify the incarnation with the virginal conception, since there is no other point at which it could have occurred.

The life-story of Jesus Christ, God and man, begins in the earliest days of his embryonic biological existence; and the significance of this fact is that the manhood which he took on is our manhood. That is, it cannot be claimed that his case was in this respect unusual, since the principle of the incarnation is that of the taking up of true, yet sinless, humanity by God. If that is the point at which his human life-line began, it is also the point at which ours begins. Such a conclusion immediately rules out any attempt to relativise the moral significance of the early stages of human life.

---

10. It is reliably reported that in the midst of a debate on Warnock in the General Synod of the Church of England a bishop sympathetic to Warnock was overheard saying 'I don't want to hear anything more about the incarnation'.

It also connects with the question of the divine image, which we have already discussed. For the reason why God could become man was that man, his creature, already bore his image; he already reflected the personal character of God in a human form. For God to become man in embryo therefore requires that man in embryo already bears the image, and absolutely forbids the possibility that in the early stages of his biological life the divine image can be absent. On the contrary, for God to become man by the miraculous fertilising of one of Mary's ova, it is necessary that a fertilised ovum should be image-bearing already and of its own nature. Man the biological entity and man the creature of God must be one. The image, with all that it implies, must be present wherever this species is to be found. The argument which seeks to divide biological man from man the image-bearer is revealed as an arbitrary, *ex post facto* attempt at the defence of an inherently indefensible proposition, namely (in Singer and Kuhse's words) that there are 'two possible senses of the term "human being"'. Within the realm of Christian discourse there can only ever be one.

The human embryo, at its earliest stage in the existence of the human being, already carries the rights and dignities which membership of this most special species entails. Biblical testimony walks hand in hand with the evidence of biology. Man in embryo is man already, and any doubt is resolved by the evidence of Scripture that the supreme man, the man who was also God, began his human existence at this point too. In our Christian thinking about 'Warnock issues', this must be our point of departure.

IN VITRO FERTILISATION: THE MAJOR ISSUES

TERESA IGLESIAS

1. The Issues

One of the fundamental critical comments that Professor Mitchell makes in his contribution to the recent *Journal of Medical Ethics* symposium[1] on *in vitro* fertilisation (IVF) is that consideration of the well-being of the child to be brought into existence by artificial methods of reproduction does not feature prominently in Professor Singer's and Mr Wells' discussion. In his reply Professor Singer seeks to rectify this impression and clarifies their position which, he says, 'rests solidly on utilitarian foundations' and 'naturally' – he adds – 'in making our utilitarian calculations, the interests of the potential child must also be taken into account'. It emerges that consideration of the well-being of the child is far from being the overriding factor in the utilitarian calculation. Even if the children generated in an artificial way will be subject to disadvantages directly attributable to that mode of generation, as long as these disadvantages are not so serious 'as to make their lives so miserable as not to be worth living' we may proceed with this mode of generation. Singer goes on to claim that it would require distinctively high 'suicide rates' to show that 'these children do not find their lives worth living'.

Singer's only way of envisaging the good of the child as it is relevant to determining the acceptability of IVF (in whatever context) and surrogate motherhood, is by way of answer to the question: would children conceived and reared in these ways get sufficient *satisfaction* out of life to prevent them committing suicide? It is clear that he lacks any objective conception of the values and goods which make for authentic human development and therefore any conception of normative conditions conducive to fostering those values and goods. The child enters the utili-

---

1. P. Singer, D. Wells, '*In vitro* fertilisation: the major issues' (with comments by G. D. Mitchell, and a response by Singer and Wells), *Journal of Medical Ethics*, 1983, 9:192-199.

tarian calculation simply as one among a number of potential points at which desires are satisfied. If, like Singer, you imagine yourself able to predict a surplus of satisfied over unsatisfied desires in the life of that child, then *there is nothing to count against* satisfying another person's desire to have that child.

Apart from (i) the well-being of the child-to-be, the other issues discussed in the symposium which I take to be major are (ii) the family's natural structure of human life (as natural as language), its relation to marriage and to the different forms of artificial parenthood, and (iii) the nature of the human embryo.

Other questions, such as the allocation of resources (and the neglected question of fertility) I take to be directly related to the general issue of the ultimate aims of medicine. In my view the essential aim of medicine is the restoration to health (or some approximation of health) of those diseased or impaired, and not the satisfaction of other needs (least of all 'needs' for which our only evidence is strong desire). On Professor Singer's conception of need there can surely be no rational way of settling resource allocation problems.

Professor Mitchell gives full consideration to the essential social dimension of the issues, particularly to the family founded on the marriage covenant as the natural context of generation. He indicates how if one followed the views and recommendations of Singer and Wells our society would be deleteriously affected. I share his point of view and believe that to be married is a fundamental condition for assuming the responsibilities of procreation, and that this is not – in moral terms – a mere matter of attitude, as we are told.

That Professor Singer's and Mr Wells' views are likely to obtain a great deal of support from medical scientists and medical practitioners is a fact too obvious to require emphasis; it shows the extent to which the prevailing medico-scientific ideology and practice have become utilitarian.

Nevertheless, it is not the case, either in theory or in practice or as a matter of tradition, that utilitarianism – in its variety of forms – is the only way or the best way to evaluate and solve our moral and social problems. Indeed, there are alternatives to the utilitarian mentality which are worth considering. My purpose here is to present one briefly. My contribution will centre around the issue I take to be basic and which deserves closer attention than was given to it in the symposium. It is an issue on which most of the other moral and social issues raised by IVF depend: the nature of the human embryo.

There are two inevitable routes that I must follow in order to tackle the problems; they can be called the *moral* and the *ontological*.

The former route issues in recognition of the values belonging to things, values which govern our behaviour and command our respect; such values as belong to things establish their *moral status*. The latter route issues in recognition of the nature of things – what they are or what the facts show of their mode of being – their *ontological status*. These two routes are interrelated, for we need to know what things are as a necessary presupposition for knowing how we should treat them, and the kind of respect owing to them.

2. The Moral Evaluation

What kind of respect is due to the human embryo? We cannot answer this question without first giving an answer to another one: what kind of respect is due to the developed human being or human person? The most basic reply we must give to this latter question may be framed in a simple principle: *no human being is property* – or what is the same – no human being can be treated as property. That some human beings have been regarded and/or treated as property by other human beings is both an historical and a current fact.

Historically, slavery best illustrates the point. The social institution of slavery made one human being, as a matter of law and practice, the property of another human being. The slave had no claim over his or her life and liberty. He could be used, exploited or even killed and so his life was of purely instrumental value. A slave, both in his life and powers, was radically a means to the interests and benefit of his master.

Currently, some have argued that infants (and even young children) are the property of their parents. So parents have the right to dispose of them if it is deemed desirable or beneficial. It is claimed that children do not have equal moral status to the fully developed human being, so they can be used for the benefit of others, as in medical experiments; to this kind of end they can be generated and subsequently disposed of. If children are property then they can be treated as property.

The abolition of slavery for every human being – including children – may be taken as one of the greatest steps in the moral development of the human family. It amounts to the recognition of the fundamental moral equality of all human beings. Indeed, human beings are not properties, objects or instruments of use to serve the benefits and interests of others. 'No human being is property' is a moral premise of our vision of man, attained through long social struggle and by the suffering lives and deaths of many individual human beings.

Recognising the radical equality of status of all members of the human family leads us also to recognise what might be meant by the principle of 'respect for persons'. This respect is a fundamental requirement of justice, in virtue of which no human being is to be used or exploited for any purpose whatsoever. It is a recognition that individually every human being at least has the right not to be used merely as means to the needs or interests of others and every innocent human being has at least the right not to be killed. 'Not to be used, not to be killed', is the ultimate moral ground where the roots of justice lie. So it is the point of departure for our dealings with one another in all the social contexts and social forms of life in which we find ourselves and which we continuously create.

The moral equality proper to all members of the human family not only pervades our international declarations and bills of rights: it is also enshrined in our laws which are designed to guarantee and protect the inviolable status of every individual human being. The equality of humans is central to the moral vision of the medical profession, in its attempt to serve life, as expressed in its codes of practice. The paramount value of each human being and the consequent moral necessity to respect it also constitutes a corner stone or first principle of traditional moral philosophies (the Kantian one being an example) as well as a corner stone of religious moral thinking and life as in, for example, the Jewish-Christian tradition. Yet, for the utilitarian tradition respect for the individual human being is not the paramount moral value; the paramount moral value is rather the realisation of some overall 'best outcome', to achieve which values and persons may be sacrificed. Accordingly, if the circumstances seem to require it, the life or lives of individual human beings may be regarded as instrumental, and expendable for that 'greater good'. Ultimately, in utilitarianism, all values can be traded off, human beings themselves can be. This is not so for the kind of non-utilitarian outlook I want to present. In this outlook any 'calculations' or weighing and comparing of values occur only on the presupposition that absolute respect for each individual human being is under no circumstances to be 'traded off', *i.e.* the direct harm or destruction of innocent human life is *never* regarded as justifiable. In this perspective all human beings are to be treated as morally equal.

Yet some non-utilitarians may ask: 'Are all human beings really equal?' 'Are we not to distinguish between the newly conceived human being – or the "potential human being" or "potential person" – and the fully developed human being, in full exercise of his or her personal capacities?'

Professor Singer and Mr Wells claim in their discussion that they 'regard the 1,2,4,8,16 or 32 cell zygote as not in the same category as a developed human being'. This means zygotes do not deserve the same moral respect accorded to the developed human being, since they are not the same kind of beings. The zygote and the developed human being differ in nature, *i.e.* in their ontological status, hence they differ in their moral status as well. Is this really so? To this question, I now turn.

3. The Nature of the Human Embryo
When philosophers and scientists study the nature of things they do so by paying attention to their material (or bodily) configuration, to their behaviour and to the powers and capacities they manifest. In other words, they find out what specific things *are* by how they appear and what they do. So if we wanted to know about the nature of the human zygote, *i.e.* what the human zygote really *is*, it would not help us to characterise it as 'genetic material' or 'biological material' (to use Singer's and Wells' phraseology, now very much used by the medical profession as well), or as something having merely 'biological life'. These expressions do not specify the particular nature of the thing they refer to. By 'genetic material' we could equally mean a segment of DNA, or some of the genes, or the chromosomes, or whole germ cells like sperm and the unfertilised ovum, or the zygote.

By 'biological material' we could mean all the above plus any somatic cell or group of cells, or organs or even the living being as a whole. The attempt to reduce the human embryo to living material of no specific kind is both scientifically and philosophically incorrect. Let us remember as well that there is no such thing as 'biological life', for life strictly speaking only occurs, is sustained and transmitted in and through individuals; and individuals are always of *specific* kinds. There is, doubtless, a pragmatic advantage in describing the newly conceived human being as 'biological' or 'genetic material'; by a mere device of language you can make it seem that there is nothing wrong in using, experimenting on, destroying, freezing and disposing of embryos – which are just 'material'.

So if we are to discern the nature of the zygote we cannot do it by reducing it to mere biological material; we need to know what particular kind of material being the zygote is by its characteristic elements, structure, organisation, inner dynamisms and capacities. We can learn much from the biological sciences in this respect. Professor Singer in one of his writings has conceded this:

> When opponents of abortion say that the embryo is a living human being from conception onwards, all they can possibly mean is that the embryo is a living member of the species *homo sapiens*. This is all that can be established as a scientific fact. But is this also the sense in which every 'human being' has 'a right to life?'[2]

(It should be noted that the expression '*homo sapiens*' is not 'neutrally scientific' and bereft of the significant moral implications that some resist in the word 'human'; it might also be noted that from a scientific viewpoint a zygote is indeed a new item in the human species, while any other cell is not.)

The fact that the zygote or embryo is a living human being from conception onwards is a sufficient reason for many to recognise that it must be treated and protected not as property but as a member of the human family. It must be respected in

---

2. W. Walters, P. Singer, eds., *Test-Tube Babies*, Oxford University Press, 1982, p. 60.

accordance with its particular life stage and condition; it must not be killed, it must not be used, instrumentalised or exploited for any purpose whatsoever. For many, including Singer and Wells, to be a human being *i.e.* a member of the human species, does not carry with it any claim on others to respect one's life. What carries this claim is the fact that a human being is in a sufficiently developed state (*i.e.* is a person) to make this claim in and through his *desire* to be so respected. Perhaps the two contrasting positions could be clarified in the following terms. The continuity of our existence as human beings, *i.e.* as members of the human species from our earliest embryonic beginnings, could be described as a dynamic process of becoming what we potentially are. This process, though, can be interpreted in two different ways: (a) as the process of development *into* a person, or (b) as the process of development *of* a person. The basic difference between these two interpretations lies in what the term 'potentially' is really taken to involve and in what is ultimately valued in human beings. Let me consider these two positions in turn.

A. *Development* into *a person*

In this approach it is maintained that we become persons, and may cease to be persons, while our existence as human beings persists all the time. Two unavoidable questions arise: (i) in virtue of what are we to be considered as persons? and (ii) at what stage of our development as human beings do we become persons?

i. Philosophers in the tradition of Locke say that a person is an organism possessing 'the concept of self as a continuing subject of experience and other mental states, and believes that it is itself such a continuing entity'.[3] In brief, self-consciousness and what goes with it is what constitutes us as persons. Within this perspective what is valued in human beings, *i.e.* that which leads us to believe that they have moral claims upon us, is the actual exercise of capacities associated with self-consciousness. It should be noted that the moral claims upon us even of full-

---

3. M. Tooley, 'Abortion and Infanticide', in M. Cohen, T. Nagel and T. Scanlon, eds., *The Rights and Wrongs of Abortion*, A Philosophy and Public Affairs Reader, Princeton, 1974, 59.

fledged persons are from this point of view not held to be absolute; for specific claims upon us (*i.e.* rights which imply correlative obligations) are not based on the simple fact of 'personhood'; rather they are based on the *express desires* of persons, which may change. So the right a person may have not to be killed is waivable if he desires to be killed. Personhood is itself not valuable; what is ultimately valuable about being a person is that you have reached that stage of development at which, having the required conceptual equipment, you are in a position to express that range of desires, satisfaction of which is alone morally significant. (Animals are capable of expressing their desires, such as the desire not to suffer pain, as much as humans are; hence, in this view, they also have rights based on those desires; they have moral claims upon us.)

ii. Those adhering to these views maintain that the particular moment at which a human being becomes a person, *i.e.* turns into a person by acquiring a concept of self and a range of other concepts necessary to having and expressing desires, is a matter of empirical determination. This determination can be left to the psychologists and is relatively unproblematic.

B. *Development* of *a person*

In this approach, in contrast with the previous one, to be a human being is to be a person. There are no stages in our existence at which this identity does not hold. If this is so, the concept of a person cannot be determined by, or restricted to, a stage – or state – of self-consciousness. Also, and as a consequence, rights are not to be founded on self-conscious desires, and so they are not necessarily connected with states of consciousness. Thus, within this outlook two questions must be answered as well: (i) if what makes someone a person is not self-consciousness, and the belief that one is that continuing self, what is it? and (ii) if fundamental rights (and obligations) are not based on conscious desires, on what are they based, and how are they related to personhood?

i. What makes us persons is the *kind of beings we are,* the kind of nature we possess, and not a passing state or stage of that kind of being. I will undertake to make good these claims in the light of two principles which for convenience may be called: the principle of unity and the principle of potentiality. By the principle of unity is meant that human beings – like any other creatures – are just one entity, one being, and not a composite of two things. They are not first physical organic bodies with (at a later stage) personhood added to them by self-consciousness, making them human beings *and* persons. They are not human organisms *first* and persons only subsequently, by virtue of the advent of a 'soul' or consciousness. Human beings are what they are on the basis of their specific organic make-up, with its proper structure, dynamism, capacities and activities. *Both* our organism and capacities are inseparably one and of a specific kind, of a 'human' kind we say, that is why we call ourselves 'human' beings. Our organic make-up, in its molecular structure (the human genes) as well as in its bodily form (the human face and hands, the human brain and feet, the human eyes) are not something separable from, or something capable of being abstracted from, the capacities they express and realise, capacities the exercise of which *is* living for us: eating, drinking, sleeping, movement from place to place, smiling, laughing, speaking a language, hoping, being open or narrow minded, pursuing ends, choosing means, adopting attitudes, determining the course of one's life. It has been rightly noted that when the idea of consciousness is completely separated from, abstracted from, humanity and human life, philosophers develop two typical syndromes, of which one is 'a dire suspicion that anything at all may be a subject of consciousness',[3] *e.g.* animals or a brain *in vitro* might be such subjects. We appropriately consider ourselves to be part of the animal kingdom because of our bodily condition. Yet our bodily condition is not something apart from what we distinctively are, with all our capacities and activities, including self-consciousness, self-determination, responsibility, love and creativity. Because of all these, we see ourselves as different from other creatures and regard ourselves as persons. We acknowledge that we are the only beings that because of our human body and capacities live and respond to reality and to others in a *personal way*. It is also in virtue of what we are as a unity of body and capacities and activities, that we regard our-

---

3. J. Teichman, 'Wittgenstein on Persons and Human Beings', *Royal Institute of Philosophy Lectures*, London, 7, 1972/1973:135-136.

selves as belonging to one and the same family, one and the same species described as *Homo sapiens*. Members of this species manifest their *personal* form of life not only individually but socially. We are the only creatures that live culturally, that manifest their higher form of life in the so called universals of culture, namely, linguistic activity, conscience, art and aesthetic appreciation, religion, political life and technology. Indeed bodily form (or organic form) and capacities are the two inseparable dimensions and determinants of any species, of any members of the animal kingdom, making them what they are in their specific nature. What things can do and how they appear is a manifestation of what they are. It is what they are that determines what they can do, not the other way around. So if we can attain self-consciousness at some stage, we must *already* be the kind of beings that can attain it. The inseparability of what a thing is and its capacities is particularly manifested in its organic continuity, in its being always the same organism. This question of continuity leads us to the principle of potentiality.

The bodily person I am now certainly began as a tiny organism of one cell, a human zygote. If this original cell was capable of developing into *me*, what capacities and potential did it have then? This is the crucial question that must be answered. The development of personal abilities (self-awareness, choice, creativity) does not come about independently of our organic development. There are no bases in reality to affirm that those capacities are 'something added' (by miracle?) at any particular stage. Thus if we are to make sense of our existence *now* as human personal beings, we must admit that whatever capacities we have now developed from what we were from the beginning. Our present abilities are only explicable if there was *always a presence* of the inherent capacity for those abilities in the human organism from the beginning. To say that only at some later stage of development do we have the *exercisable* abilities of self-consciousness and self-determination, while true, *leaves unexplained* the origin and development of these abilities; and the failure to recognise the need for explanation at this point results in failure to acknowledge the nature of the *subject* to which the abilities belong. The value of a being is indeed related to the things into which it can develop, but not independently of, but precisely because of what the being *is*. For the actual capacity to achieve a particular type of development must always have been present prior to development, and is therefore significant in determining what kind of being we are dealing with, even in the earliest stages of its existence.

We know that a new human individual organism with the internal potential to develop into an adult, given nurture, comes into existence as a result of the process of fertilisation at conception. We must reckon then that such a potential is an *actually present capacity* which in the normal course of development will come to be more or less fully manifested in the personal life of an adult. Hence, the *kind* of life that the zygote has, because of the capacity it presently possesses, is *personal* life, *i.e.* the life of a personal being or a personal subject. It is this presence of personal capacities – which must be attributable to a personal subject – that makes a difference between one kind of life (that of human persons) and another (that of say, dogs). It must also be noted that living entities are not machines built up out of blocks. The development of a living entity, *becoming* what it is *capable* of being, is indeed a process, but the entity itself and its *coming to be*, is not. At any particular time, the entity is *in toto* or is not at all (this is an important consideration for the debate about brain death as well). For living human beings are not like, for example, clocks, that progressively come to be and can be assembled and dismantled. Whereas you can reasonably speak of having half a clock, you cannot reasonably speak of having half a person.

ii. Let us now turn to the question of basic rights. It is in virtue of what things are that we treat them one way or another; it is in virtue of what human beings are, right from the beginning of their existence, that they must be accorded absolute respect and their lives treated as inviolable. Rights are based on values, and values on the recognition of what things are. The ultimate ground of value is being, not passing states of beings, like activities and desires; for these are the manifestations of what the being is. What one can become is a possibility based on what one is. Becoming has its only basis in being. Every potentiality must be based on something actual, on a real actuality. Basic rights (and obligations), like the right not to be killed and the obligation not to kill an innocent human being, are based on what human beings are, not on particular states of conscious desires. Thus from this perspective what is valued in human beings is *themselves*, what they are, and not just what they achieve.

4. What is Morally Desirable

In the strictest sense IVF is not a medical problem, *i.e.* a problem arising from concern for health and the development of means to restore or improve health. Rather it is one of an increasing number of biotechnical problems *i.e.* problems arising from the development of techniques designed to circumvent or modify existing (usually defective) modes of bodily function. These biotechnical developments along with other scientific developments 'threaten to turn *Homo sapiens* into *Homo mechanicus*' as has recently been noted.[4] Although this is a general point, it is one of great significance in relation to the direction medicine is now taking. It cannot be ignored in our evaluations of medical progress and development.

Having said that, let me turn to our main question. What kind of respect is due to the human embryo? Is the human embryo to be protected as a human being or as property? The only possible answer, in the light of the considerations advanced in the previous section, is that respect due to the human embryo must not differ *in kind* from the respect due to any other human being; the human embryo must be protected as a human being, not as a property or an object of use. This means that the human embryo has the right not to be killed and not to be used or exploited for any purpose whatsoever.

This makes clear that a form of study which risks harm to human embryos and experimentation on human embryos for scientific purposes is immoral. Such experiments are never in the interest of the subject experimented upon, who is harmed, used up and destroyed, always being treated radically as a means, as an object of use, as a 'product', as 'material' – to use favourite dehumanising terms in vogue in the literature.

In the context of alleviating infertility, a number of spare embryos are generated as the most economic procedure for at-

---

4. Sir I. Jakobovits, 'Jewish Medical Ethics - a brief overview', *Journal of Medical Ethics*, 1983, 9:112.

taining the general aim in view – the greater chances of pregnancy with the minimum of effort, expense and trauma. Yet the well-being and existence of each individual life thus generated is made secondary and as such instrumental to the general aim. Those lives, if not required for the desired pregnancy, will be disposed of, used for experiments, or frozen until a time comes when they will be in demand for implantation, experimentation or disposal. The common practice of superovulation clearly involves an immoral instrumentalisation of the embryo.

Nature 'prodigally' disposes of large numbers of embryos, even without their being noticed by the women who carry them, we are told. Hence, some ask, if nature is so prodigal with so many embryos, why are we not entitled to generate some that can be used for the benefit of others or of science, and when required destroyed, or disposed of? First, it should be remarked that even if it were true that many embryos die naturally that would not be a fact which told us what kind of being the embryo *is,* and so what kind of respect is owed to it. Second, natural processes such as floods, droughts, volcanic eruptions and other kinds of natural disasters are natural processes as much as the processes whereby the loss of fertilised ova naturally occur. These processes cannot be taken as indicative of what we are to do, of the actions we are to choose. To think otherwise is to ignore the fact that what we intend, decide and deliberately bring about are *not* (in this sense) natural processes (and just because they are not, we are answerable for them). Hence they cannot be measured against the results that nature brings about. We are moral beings. Physical nature is not.

Irreparable damage to the embryo or the child-to-be is a feature of IVF procedures which cannot be excluded. This is clearly acknowledged by, for example, Dr Edwards, when he mentions the back-up methods of monitoring abnormalities after IVF and implantations, and suggests *in vitro* abortion.[5] This risk is implicitly recognised by the recent Royal College of Obstetricians and Gynaecologists' (RCOG) report on IVF when it claims 'the possibility that a child born with an abnormality might in due course be able to sue its parents and

---

5. R. G. Edwards, J. M. Purdy, eds., *Human Conception* in vitro, London, 1982, 372-373.

the doctors cannot be ruled out'.[6] We are not morally justified in directly engaging in bringing about such risk of harm. In natural procreation an abnormal embryo might or might not abort. In the IVF process it must be destroyed. In natural procreation the child is conceived and received unconditionally 'for better or for worse'; in the IVF programme only conditionally 'for better', so primarily not for his or her own sake, but the satisfaction of a desire. It needs to be recognised that the well-being of the child should be of paramount importance – as that of any other human being; recognition should be embodied in attitudes and practices which exclude treating the child as a commodity, a property or mere object of satisfaction at any stage of his or her existence.

One should welcome the fact that Singer and Wells recognise that secrecy over gamete donation (as may occur in artificial insemination by donor (AID) or in surrogate motherhood) need not be maintained. Openness will indeed encourage greater responsibility and attitudes of trust and truth in all those involved. Yet meeting the requirements of openness hardly meets all the objections of these practices. The practices not only put the well-being of the child at risk but surrogate motherhood in particular involves a direct instrumentalisation of the feminine power of gestation. The phrase 'rent-a-womb' fairly aptly characterises the instrumentalisation in question; for whether one pays or not, the woman's body becomes usable accommodation. Neither children born or unborn, nor women, nor the rest of mankind are ever to be property, but beings to be respected, cared for and loved for their own sake, and not with a view to achieving other purposes. We all have to grow in that rare virtue that men of great stature have shown: to love human beings just because they are human beings.

6. *Report of the Royal College of Obstetricians and Gynaecologists Ethics Committee on in vitro fertilisation and embryo replacement or transfer*, London, 1983, Sec. 10,7.

THE ETHICS OF EXPERIMENTATION

RICHARD HIGGINSON

During recent years, and particularly since the publication of the Warnock Report, there has been much discussion about the morality of performing experiments on early embryos. In this paper, I want to set that discussion within a wider context which has too often been avoided in the debate, namely, the question of performing experiments on human beings in general.

In 1964 the World Medical Association drew up a code of ethics on human experimentation, which was revised in 1975 as the Declaration of Helsinki.[1] It includes the following recommendations: that biomedical research involving human subjects cannot legitimately be carried out unless the importance of the objective is in proportion to the inherent risk to the subject; that every biomedical research project involving human subjects should be preceded by a careful assessment of predictable risks in comparison with the foreseeable benefits to the subject or to others; that concern for the interests of the subject must always prevail over the interests of science and society; that each potential subject must be adequately informed of the aims, methods, anticipated benefits and potential hazards of the study and the discomfort it may entail; that consent should be freely given, informed and preferably in writing; that in cases of legal incompetence, informed consent for the research project should be obtained from the legal guardian in accordance with national legislation; and that where physical or mental incapacity makes it impossible to obtain informed consent, or when the subject is a minor, permission from the responsible relative replaces that of the subject in accordance with national legislation.

The Declaration makes a distinction between medical research in which the aim is essentially diagnostic or therapeutic for a patient, and research in which the essential object is purely scientific and without direct diagnostic or therapeutic value to the person subjected to the research. This distinction is often called

---

1. This code may conveniently be found in *The Handbook of Medical Ethics*, BMA, London, 1981.

that between therapeutic and non-therapeutic research. But even with regard to the latter, it is emphasised that it is the duty of the doctor to remain the protector of the life and health of the person concerned; that the subjects should be volunteers; that the investigator(s) should discontinue the research if he or they judge that it may, if continued, be harmful to the individual; and that in research on man, the interest of science and society should never take precedence over considerations related to the well-being of the subject.

There is an element of ambiguity concerning these detailed (if overlapping) recommendations on non-therapeutic research, since the statement that the subjects should be volunteers is not qualified by the reservation that is applied to experimentation in general, that where potential subjects are legally incompetent or physically or mentally incapacitated permission may be given by a legal guardian or responsible relative. One is thus left in some doubt as to whether proxy consent is deemed applicable to non-therapeutic research, where the benefits of research are less likely to rebound to the advantage of the individual concerned and where a greater measure of selfless altruism appears to be involved. There are some ethicists who would argue that the Declaration should be interpreted strictly and that non-therapeutic research should not be done by proxy consent. At the time when he was writing *The Patient as Person,* the American ethicist Paul Ramsey argued this forcibly with regard to experiments on children. He wrote thus:

> To attempt to consent for a child to be made an experimental subject is to treat a child as not a child. It is to treat him as if he were an adult person who has consented to become a joint adventurer in the common cause of medical research. If the grounds for this are alleged to be the presumptive or implied consent of the child, that must simply be characterised as a violent and a false presumption. Non-therapeutic, non-diagnostic experimentation involving human subjects must be based on true consent if it is to proceed as a human enterprise. No child or incompetent adult can choose to become a participating member of medical undertakings, and no one else on earth should decide to subject these people to investigations having no relation to their own treatment. That

is a canon of loyalty to them . . . when he is grown, the child may put away childish things and become a true volunteer.[2]

On the whole, however, ethicists, doctors, scientists and lawmakers have not taken as rigorous a view as Ramsey. They have interpreted the Helsinki Declaration as allowing non-therapeutic research on children by proxy consent. A fellow-American ethicist who took issue with Paul Ramsey was Richard McCormick.[3] McCormick argued that parental consent for non-therapeutic research is acceptable when, like therapeutic research, it is a reasonable presumption of the child's wishes. Children may reasonably be presumed to wish the welfare of others, as long as this does not take place at undue cost to themselves. They may thus be presumed to approve an experiment upon themselves that is not in any realistic way to their harm, and represents a potentially great benefit to other people. Ramsey argued that we should not presume a child's charity, which comes by 'grace' and 'moral maturity', but McCormick said that the experiments he had in mind were works of social justice, not supererogation. He too would rule out experiments involving notable risk, discomfort and inconvenience.

In favour of Ramsey's stringent position is his ardent zeal that we do not exploit for our own interest those who have no voice. Once non-therapeutic research on children has been allowed at all, the dangers of exploitation, of sliding down a slippery and increasingly hazardous slope, are ever with us. Against it, and in favour of McCormick's more permissive position, is an equally genuine concern for children's welfare; for children's pathology is sufficiently distinctive that they ultimately stand to lose if no non-therapeutic research is done on them. If the caveats which McCormick and the Helsinki Declaration insist upon are observed then the children who are subject to research *ought* to be safe from exploitation, since experiments involving notable risk would be ruled out, and where the experiments un-

2. Paul Ramsey, *The Patient as Person*, New Haven & London, 1970, p. 14.
3. See McCormick's article 'Proxy Consent in the Experimentation Situation', reprinted in *How Brave a New World? Dilemmas in Bioethics*, London, 1981, ch. 4.

expectedly turned out to threaten harm, they would be discontinued. This is a very big 'if', and constant vigilance needs to be exercised in and upon the medical and scientific communities to ensure that these conditions are being observed, but *if* they are, I am happy to accept the position adopted by McCormick, for it seems right to view children, like adults, as having responsibilities as well as rights – or one might say, as being social creatures as well as individuals.

Like McCormick, I would be prepared to adopt the same position with regard to experiments on fetuses as I would towards experimentation on children.[4] In other words, non-therapeutic research is permissible so long as there is no significant risk to the fetus or, of course, the mother. It may be that no research which has been or will be contemplated can meet this condition, but it is a matter of honesty and logic to state what one's attitude is in *principle*. If objections are going to be made against a proposed or existing course of action, we need to be very careful about exactly what those objections are.

What this lengthy prolegomenon on experimentation is leading to is as follows. My objection to experiments being done on early embryos does not rest on the argument that the experiment lacks their informed consent, because I am already willing to accept proxy consent in the cases of children (in practice) and fetuses (in principle).

The objection is based fairly and squarely on the nature of the harm done to the embryo concerned. Such harm is not unlikely, insignificant or insubstantial. It is harm with a capital H – wounding, malignant and deadly. Hardly any embryos which have been subjected to experimentation will be permitted long to survive the experience, even if they have emerged from the actual experiment alive. Such experimentation is equally objectionable whatever form it takes – whether it is a case of the embryo being manipulated, dissected or simply observed. Even where the embryo is simply being observed, the embryo is in a position analogous to that of a prisoner being watched in his cell, with the hangman's noose or the electric chair a certain destiny at the end of his period of confinement – or so it will be

4. McCormick's article 'Public Policy and Fetal Research' is reprinted as ch. 5 of *How Brave A New World?*

if the recommendation of the Warnock Report, that no live human embryo derived from *in vitro* fertilisation may be kept alive if not transferred to a woman beyond 14 days after fertilisation, becomes law.[5] Even where the embryo is simply being observed, its own interests and welfare have been completely lost to view. In contravention of the Helsinki Declaration, the alleged interests of science and society have clearly taken precedence over considerations relating to the well-being of the research subject – with fatal consequences for the latter.

As presented so far, there is of course a missing step in my argument. I have assumed that human embryos possess the same status as human fetuses, or children, or for that matter adults. I have assumed that we should treat them with the same respect, and therefore refrain from any experiment upon them which is likely to cause them harm. I will now try to fill in that missing step in the argument.

In my reading and listening upon this subject, I have become aware of four reasonably distinct positions on the status of the human embryo. (When I speak of the embryo henceforth I have in mind the embryo at its earliest stage, the first 14 days after fertilisation. I am aware that the proper technical word for this stage is the zygote, but embryo seems to pass as a popular shorthand.) The four positions are these:

(1) the embryo at this stage is a human person;
(2) the embryo at this stage may be a human person – we cannot be sure;
(3) the embryo at this stage is a potential human person, 'potential' being used in a sense which stresses continuity with the actual human person who emerges later;
(4) the embryo at this stage is a potential human person, 'potential' being used in a sense which stresses *dis*continuity with the actual human person who emerges later.

It is my conviction that if one holds any of positions (1) to (3), one ought to be committed to respecting the rights and preserving the life of the early embryo. If one holds position (4) it

5. See paragraph 11.22 on p. 66 of the *Report of the Committee of Inquiry into Human Fertilisation and Embryology* (hereafter cited as *Warnock Report*).

is understandable that one is not so committed, but position (4) is one that no intelligent person, grappling seriously and honestly with the evidence before him, ought to be in the business of holding anyway. Let us go through these positions one by one.

The first position, that the early embryo is already a human person, is one that I hold myself. I have argued for this position in other places (and this position has already been expounded in an excellent way by Dr Teresa Iglesias) so I will avoid a duplication of material at this point.[6] Clearly if one does adopt this position, full protection for the early embryo naturally follows. It is not surprising that those who hold this position tend to be the most ardent opponents of embryo research.

The second position is more agnostic. It recognises that there are certain plausible grounds for regarding the early embryo as a person, but perceives certain counter-arguments which militate against that position. In the face of conflicting evidence which appears incapable of satisfactory resolution, the person who holds this position feels that it is best to humbly admit uncertainty and to say: 'I'm not sure'. An example of such a person is the aforementioned Richard McCormick. For him the large number of spontaneous early abortions and the phenomena of twinning and recombination raise 'doubts and questions' about ascribing personhood to embryos in the pre-implantation period.[7] I do not myself believe that these phenomena pose insuperable problems to regarding the early embryo as a person, but instead of trying to answer those questions and remove those doubts, let us consider the moral implications of taking this position where one frankly admits one's uncertainty. Does this position provide *carte blanche* for performing experiments on early embryos? Surely not. Let us consider the analogous situation of a man charged with the task of demolishing a disused building, doubtless with some very good end in view (like the construction of a new building). When he arrives at the site the man does not know whether anybody (*e.g.*, a small child or a tramp) is inside the building or not. Someone may be there,

6. See Teresa Iglesias, '*In vitro* fertilisation: the major issues', *Journal of Medical Ethics*, 1984, 1, reprinted above, ch. 2.
7. See McCormick, *How Brave A New World?*, p. 182.

someone may not. Perhaps the chances are that no-one is. Nevertheless, there is surely a moral duty incumbent on the demolition expert to make absolutely sure that no-one is inside, before he sets fire to it or collapses it or uses whatever is his preferred method of demolition. If he failed to carry out a check and a small child or tramp was killed as a result, it would be a very limp excuse for the demolition expert to say 'I wasn't sure that there was a person there'.

I recognise that this is not a perfect analogy because the possibility of finding out for sure that no person was present was open to the demolition expert, in a way which is not true for the would-be experimenter. Nevertheless, the principle of caution, of unwillingness to take precipitate action which *might* endanger the life of a fellow-human, surely holds good. There is something strange and sinister about the way in which those who profess ambiguity on the status of the early embryo often assume that this allows freedom to carry out research. We do well to ponder the words of Oliver O'Donovan:

> If we should wish to charge our own generation with crimes against humanity because of this experimental research, I would suggest that the crime should not be the old-fashioned crime of killing babies, but the new and subtle crime of making babies to be ambiguously human, of presenting to us members of our own species who are doubtfully proper objects of compassion and love.[8]

The doubts may of course be very genuine ones, but to those who harbour them I would plead with all my heart: give the embryo the benefit of the doubt.

The third position purports to be clear in not regarding the embryo as a person, yet seeks to do justice to the promise contained within the embryo even at this early stage. It speaks of a 'potential human person' as opposed to a 'human person with potential', a phrase which advocates of position (1) may be happy to use. Advocates of this third position see personhood as a state of being (and with that status) which is acquired at some later stage of development. This stage may be a certain point in the development of the embryo (*e.g.*, implantation, the formation of the primitive streak, the onset of consciousness in the

---

8. Oliver O'Donovan, *Begotten or Made?*, Oxford,1984, p. 65.

formation of the cerebral cortex), of the fetus (*e.g.*, quickening, viability) or of the child (birth, perhaps even the onset of ability to communicate articulately). Probably most adherents to this third position would reject one of these later stages and opt for a certain point in the development of the embryonic brain – and depending on precisely which point this means that personhood is deemed to be acquired anything from 3 weeks to 24 weeks after fertilisation.[9] Other adherents to this position simply remain agnostic about the point when personhood becomes reality.

Again I ask the question: does this position provide *carte blanche* for performing experiments on early embryos? Again my answer is: surely not. Interestingly, the expression of dissent by the minority group on the Warnock Committee who objected to any use of human embryos in research was based upon acceptance of position (3). Here I quote what they wrote:

> The special status of the human embryo and the protection to be afforded to it by law do not in our view depend upon the decision as to when it becomes a person. Clearly, once that status has been accorded all moral principles and legal enactments which relate to persons will apply. But before that point has been reached the embryo has a special status because of its potential for development to a stage at which everyone would accord it the status of a human person. It is in our view wrong to create something with the potential for becoming a human person and then deliberately to destroy it.[10]

In other words, we take the potential of the early embryo seriously. We pay it the greatest respect in view of the capacity which is so much prized (*e.g.*, capacity to feel, respond and think) and into which he or she (sexual identity having been already decided) is growing moment by moment. We do not regard the embryo as some static entity, but as a creature in a fluid and dynamic process of development. We adopt a historical perspective and think about the future (the embryo's possible future, that is, not somebody else's future) rather than the pre-

---

9. *E.g.*, the majority group on the Church of England Board of Social Responsibility Working Party on Human Fertilisation and Embryology took this view, and opted for a point around 40 days after conception. See their report *Personal Origins*, CIO, London, 1985, ch. 3.
10. *Warnock Report*, p. 90.

sent alone.

This is what we do with human life outside the womb. Let me use another analogy. Consider a country with a long tradition of democracy which is taken over by a totalitarian ruler. He makes the country into a one-party state and people lose their rights to vote. Which people lose their right to vote? Firstly, obviously, the men and women who were already exercising that vote during the years when the country was a democracy. But the boys and girls who have not yet exercised that vote because they weren't old enough have also, in a very real sense, lost their vote. If the totalitarian system remains in existence indefinitely, they too have been deprived of their rights. They may not *feel* the loss as much, since they have never personally known what it was like to vote; and yet the fact remains – assuming one grants that democracy is a more just system than totalitarianism – that these youngsters at the time of the take-over have been victims of injustice. In a similar way, an embryo who does not *feel* the pain of being experimented upon and killed can be a victim of the most serious form of injustice: undeserved death.

Unfortunately, many who adhere to position (3) do not treat the notion of potential with the seriousness which is implicit within that position. I say 'implicit' because when they describe *actual* personhood as being present at some later stage they usually still depend largely on the language of potential for affirming the importance of what is actually present. If they say that the embryo becomes an actual person when the brain flickers into consciousness, what is exciting them is the potential harboured within that brain. The brain is associated with characteristically 'human' or 'personal' qualities like rationality, moral responsibility or spiritual awareness. But the seven- or eight-week old embryo is still very far from being a rational, morally responsible and spiritually aware human being. It is potentially all that – just as it was potentially all that at the one- or two-week old stage. It has simply scaled more of the obstacles to realising its potential by the later stage – like the danger of failing to implant.

Alternatively, advocates of position (3) may argue that personhood is not acquired until the moment of birth. Physical independence of its mother is regarded as the key criterion for ascribing personhood. The notion of independence is regarded as all-important. But again one may ask: how real at that stage is such independence? For many months after birth the baby is hopelessly dependent upon a mother or some human substitute for a mother. It has no more ability to fend for itself for food, clothing and shelter than it did during its nine months of sojourn in the womb. Again the description of actual personhood has a large measure of potential language written into it.

My argument is this: if advocates of position (3) were *consistent* in their talk of respecting potential, then they would be forced to go back behind the point at which they ascribe personhood (be it brain development or birth) and protect the human embryo from the earliest stages of its existence.

Finally, we come to the fourth position. This may also use the language of potential, but it does so in a significantly different sense than the advocates of position (3).

Advocates of this fourth position are strident in their attempts to emphasise the gulf between the early embryo and the human person as normally understood. Often the language of 'potential human beings' is actually abandoned, and what is spoken of instead is 'living tissue' or 'a bundle of cells'.[11] Nevertheless, the potential of this so-called bundle of cells would not actually be denied.

The difference between advocates of positions (3) and (4) may be expounded thus. Advocates of position (3) are recognising what one might call built-in potential. They are recognising potential in a way similar to how we view apple-trees in the winter-time: as having the potential for foliage and fruit. The potential for growth is contained within the embryo as it is the apple-tree. All that is required in each case are a supply of nutrients and a favourable environment. We will then see a realisation of the potential which is already contained within. In contrast, advocates of position (4) understand potential in a way similar to the relationship between a building site and a housing estate. The one does have potential for the other, but it is not built-in; without deliberate acts of human creativity, the building site will remain uninhabitable. Advocates of this position often

---

11. As, *e.g.*, in the opinions expressed in the press and on the media by Mr Robert Winston of the Hammersmith Hospital.

obscure the issue by saying that sperm and eggs, like the embryo, are alive and also have potential. In fact, this illustration serves to highlight the two very different uses of the word 'potential'. Sperm and eggs do have potential, but on their own that potential will never be realised; the supreme act of human creativity is necessary to realise the potential by bringing the two together. The relationship between sperm and eggs, on the one hand, and the human person on the other, is analogous to that between a building site and building materials on the one hand, and a finished housing estate on the other. But once we have created a human embryo, and put it within a suitable environment, it realises its own potential. It is like a house that builds itself. That is the nature of the embryo's potential. There is no great gulf between what the early embryo is and what we all recognise as the human person is; to say so is to judge in the shallowest possible manner by superficial appearances, and without any honest attention to the processes involved.

Again I cite the dissenting group on the Warnock Committee:

> It may be argued that the ovum and sperm also have the potential for becoming a human person and yet their loss at menstruation and ejaculation or by experimentation is accepted. It is true that the ovum and sperm are genetically unique but neither alone, even in the most favourable environment, will develop into a human person. They do not have this potential. The embryo, on the other hand, given the appropriate environment, will develop to the stage at which there would be general agreement that the status of a person be accorded to it. It must therefore be given special protection so that this potential can normally be fulfilled.[12]

In line with this reasoning the group recommended that nothing be done that would reduce the chance of successful implantation of the embryo.

My challenge to advocates of position (4) is therefore different to my challenge to advocates of positions (2) and (3). To those who falsely try to distance themselves from what they once were, to those who misguidedly or maliciously equate sperm and eggs on the one hand with human embryo on the other, I say: stop pulling the wool over your own and other

12. *Warnock Report*, p. 91.

people's eyes. Recognise the continuity in human development, and stop basing your arguments extolling the excusability of experiments on embryos on the false presumption that this continuity does not exist.

Before I leave position (4) I would like to answer a point made by Dr Patrick Steptoe in a debate in which I was recently involved with him, at the Cambridge Union, a point which I believe has also been made by others who are active in this field of embryo research. Their argument is that the embryos ('fertilised eggs of human origin' – Steptoe) on which experiments are done are 'no-hopers', *i.e.* embryos which are known to be defective and which would have no hope of survival if implanted in a human womb. Because they are already doomed, what does it matter if we hasten their end a little and in the process accumulate some useful knowledge by performing experiments on them? In reply to this, I would like to make 3 points.

(1) If the embryo is doomed to perish soon, should we not respect its right to a peaceful death? We do not use the fact that certain elderly patients are racked by terminal cancer as a *carte blanche* for performing lethal experiments on them.

(2) If the researchers stumbled across a spare embryo which was not defective in any way, but would - if implanted in a suitable environment - have a fair chance of development, would they feel inhibited about doing research on it? One suspects not. Indeed, the Warnock Committee by the smallest of majorities approved the creation of embryos specifically for research purposes. These would involve many healthy embryos, and for certain types of research, that is precisely the sort of embryo which is required. Furthermore, it would almost certainly be impossible to draw a clear-cut distinction in law between embryos which do have a chance of survival (on which experiments should not be done) and embryos which do not (on which they may).

(3) My suspicion that the would-be researchers have their eyes on some quite viable embryos is confirmed by the fact that other scientists involved in embryo research whom I have heard speak would like freedom to do experiments considerably beyond the 14-day limit stipulated by Warnock. I have heard one

such scientist suggest 28 days. If an embryo can survive to 28 days it may not be such a 'no-hoper' after all. Again, one suspects a certain amount of pulling the wool over people's eyes by the research contingent.

In conclusion, I would like to make three comments about the form this argument has taken. First, I realise that some may object that my argument is one-sided, in that it concentrates single-mindedly on the rights and interests of the embryo and does not balance against those benefits to other people which may arguably accrue from research. I do not deny that these benefits may be numerous and they may be considerable, although most remain highly hypothetical and sometimes these alleged benefits are described in a misleading way, *e.g.*, *eliminating* embryos with genetic defects sometimes closeted together with *curing* embryos with genetic defects. But let us suppose for a moment the benefits are substantial and appear to bring unmitigated good. Does that make the research which has produced the benefits justifiable? Hardly. Many substantial benefits might accrue from performing lethal experiments on you and me, but our precious dignity as human beings would have been terminally violated in the process. *We* are fortunate enough to be able to seek shelter under the Helsinki Declaration, and in particular the provision that the interests of science and society should never take precedence over considerations relating to the well-being of the human subject. The argument of this paper has been that if we exercise moral logic coolly and compassionately, we are duty bound to offer the same protection to the early embryo.

Secondly, I would like to say something about the *philosophical* preference which my stance on the ethics of experimentation reflects. Most of those who support embryo research are – wittingly or unwittingly – utilitarians. They believe that there is justification in sacrificing the interests of the individual in order to serve the interests (usually interpreted as increase the happiness) of the greatest number. Now I am not one of those who believe that utilitarianism is a dirty word at which we should take a routine spit every time it is mentioned. In many circumstances I am sure that it is right that what serves the interests and happiness of the majority should take precedence over what serves the interests and happiness of the minority. Anyone who supports a democratic form of government is bound to be a utilitarian to some extent. But as a *sole* approach to moral decision-making utilitarianism is inadequate and dangerous. For pure utilitarianism leaves minorities in a terribly vulnerable position *vis-à-vis* majorities (as the experience of Jews and mentally handicapped people in Nazi Germany makes clear). It is important that alongside our concern for the maximisation of human happiness we place a commensurate stress on safeguarding the rights and dignity of the individual. This emphasis will serve to qualify a utilitarian approach and prevent it being abused, because it will insist that there are some things, like the taking of innocent life, which should never be done even though they may seem to serve the interests of the majority. The Helsinki Declaration seeks to provide such safeguards, just as do United Nations Declarations of Human Rights. This concern for individual rights and dignity is one that has – in the past – had solid backing both in philosophical and theological tradition. The great Enlightenment philosopher Immanuel Kant expressed such a concern when he said 'Always treat every person as an end in himself, never merely as a means'; while Christian theologians have found support for it in the loving concern God shows for the individual, the precious dignity which attaches to each individual as someone created in the image of God, someone for whom Christ died, someone whom God calls by name, someone who if lost or outcast or thought of little account is of *special* concern to God, and about whose well-being and salvation God is so concerned that for the moment the well-being of 99 others slides into the background. It is in seeking to be true to this important strand in ethical thinking that I cannot go along with the purely utilitarian approach which lends support to embryo research.

My third comment is this. Readers may be surprised that I have not used more specifically *Christian* considerations to bolster my argument, nor have I based a large part of my argument on the conviction that the early embryo actually is a human person. This is so despite the fact that I believe (as my final comments have indicated) that Christian considerations *do* bolster the argument, and that I am genuinely convinced that the early embryo *is* a person. The reason that my argument has taken the form which it has is that I believe we need to use arguments which are likely to persuade people of all beliefs or none, and that the case for prohibiting experiments on embryos can be plausibly put even to those who are not convinced of the embryo's actual personhood, *i.e.*, those who simply think that the embryo may be a person, or is a potential one. I have argued that protection should be given to the embryo on the grounds of natural justice. And who knows, in arguing on these predominantly secular grounds I may even have won to the cause some of you who are Christians.

SOME THEOLOGICAL PERSPECTIVES ON THE HUMAN EMBRYO

DAVID ATKINSON

The purpose of this paper is to lay out some biblical themes which contribute to a theological account of the status of the human embryo, an account which itself is part of the information needed for Christian moral judgements in the problem areas of human embryology. Our task, in other words, is a limited one. We will not stray very far into the wider task of Christian ethics, nor deal with the equally important pastoral considerations, particularly concerning the alleviating or circumventing of infertility, which have rightly brought these themes into prominence recently.

The Shape of Christian Ethics

We begin with some remarks on the shape of Christian ethics, and do so by referring first to the ancient story of God's covenant with Noah.

After the story of the Flood, the narrator of Genesis 9:1-7 concentrates on two main questions. First, he is concerned with the disordered state of the present world, and how human life is to be ordered within it. And second, he speaks of the covenant blessing of God on the life that has been saved, and of the restriction on certain aspects of human behaviour without which God's blessing cannot be enjoyed. Let us look at these in turn.

Verse 1 is a conscious echo of the creation story: 'Be fruitful and multiply and fill the earth.' However, the tone is different: fear and dread (v. 2) now colour this renewed command. In the context of a severe disruption and degeneration of the creation, which came originally from God's hands, 'very good', God restates his creation purpose. In a sense, God is giving creation a new start, but the context is one of abnormality. Everything has been radically disrupted through the Fall. The Flood story speaks of divine judgement on human wickedness. But still God does not abandon his purposes for humankind. The abnormality remains, however. This is seen in the different ways God's will is expressed, first in Genesis 1 and 2, and now in a world which has been disordered. God's man is no longer in the Garden of Eden.

The importance of stressing this point is both to say that our lives and our decision-making share in this abnormality, and therefore also to say that we must beware of making morally normative whatever happens empirically to be the case. We cannot simply read off the way things are or ought to be by empirical criteria and scientific observation. Sin has disordered the way things are. It has also distorted our perceptions. Even were we still in the Garden, we would need the instruction of the divine word of revelation in order to understand the true nature and purpose of created things. How much more this side of the Fall! We must be very careful for example not to try to read off the true nature of what living human entities are, or ought to be, by genetic criteria alone.

So the context for human living is no longer 'very good'. This new start after the Flood, marked by fear and dread, is also coloured by the breach of covenant between human beings and God. The sin recorded in Genesis 3 leads to the perversity which needed the cleansing judgement of the Flood. But now God is establishing the conditions under which life may again be lived in covenant with him. Life is now a struggle, and God imposes certain constraints on it.

Thus all Christian ethical decision-making takes place within a tension. We know something of the 'proper' will of God in creation, and yet know that this will comes to us 'refracted' through the disorders of the world. There is a further tension, too: we are, to use New Testament terms, still 'in Adam' as well as being 'in Christ'. In other words, while we are no longer in the Garden of Eden, we are not yet in the New Heaven and the New Earth.

It should be no surprise, therefore, that some of the ethical dilemmas which press themselves on us may require of us actions that we would not take if we were in 'the Garden', or if Christ's kingdom had already fully come. The very existence of conflicting moral claims is itself an indication and symptom of the fallenness of this world order. There may be some situations in which we cannot act in a way that is wholly good and wholly free from guilt. We may find ourselves needing to work with a hierarchy of moral claims, and needing to evaluate lesser evils and greater goods.

Innocent Human Life
Having said that, and moving now to the second of our author's concerns in Genesis 9, we are given certain principles to guide our moral priorities. We need to note the nature of the restrictions imposed on human beings by God if they are to enjoy the divine blessing. There is first a blessing on all creation (vv. 9-10) as God establishes his covenant. This indicates that all life, animal and human, is significant to God. Even animal blood may not be needlessly shed. The affirmation that animal life is significant to God is illustrated by the restriction against the tendency to bloodthirstiness implicit in the command, 'You shall not eat flesh with its life, that is its blood.' (v.4). Animal blood may only be shed within restricted bounds. 'Even when man slaughters and kills, he is to know that he is touching something which, because it is life, is in a special manner God's property; and as a sign of this he is to keep his hands off the blood'.[1]

But more than this: the blood of human beings is not to be shed at all. One human being may not decide to take the life of another. God's lordship over all human life is here asserted. There is a blessing on all saved from the Flood, yet there is a distinction between the restricted killing of animals, and the strong prohibition against killing fellow human beings. It is only the utterly serious occasion of murder among fallen humankind which, in our author's mind, can ever require one human being by divine command to take the life of another. The death penalty in this passage only belongs within an overriding respect for the inviolability of human life. And that is a principle which is elaborated elsewhere throughout the Bible: a prohibition against shedding innocent human blood (*cf.*, *e.g.*, Num. 35:31-4; Is. 59:7; Jer. 22:3; Matt. 27:4).

In summary, the Flood story points us to these themes:

> i. We cannot simply read off the full nature of the way things are or ought to be by scientific criteria alone. We need rather to place our understanding of scientific data within the

1. G. von Rad, *Genesis*, London, 1972[3].

context of a created order, in which facts come to us laden with value from the Creator's hands.

ii. There is a value on all life as such, human and animal; there are restrictions on the taking of any life.

iii. There is distinction between the human species and other animals with respect to the degree of protection appropriate to them.

iv. There is also absolute prohibition against the shedding of innocent human blood, namely the principle that innocent human beings have an inviolable right not to be deliberately killed.

The reason for the particular respect accorded to the human species is given in Genesis 9:6, 'for God made man in his own image'.

The Divine Image

In the light of what we have said above, the question presses: what counts as an innocent human being in the sense that such a being has a right not to be deliberately killed? Let us explore this by taking further the concept of the divine image.

The first point to note is that there is a range of interpretations of the meaning of the *imago Dei*. Man's upright stature, his moral nature, his capacity to know God, his rationality, his status of dominion over the rest of creation, his sexuality as male and female in interpersonal communion – all have been candidates. And in a sense, all of these are aspects of the expression of the divine image. However, most of these concentrate on some capacity in human beings to do or to be certain things. By contrast, the consensus of interpreters these days would, I think, agree with Westermann's view:

> The image is not a question of a quality in people but of the fact that God has created people as his counterpart and that human beings can have a history with God. The image of God is only there in the relationship of God and the individual.[2]

This relational aspect to the 'image' underlies also Paul's use of the analogy of the mirror: 'We all beholding as in a mirror

2. C. Westermann.

the glory of the Lord are being changed into his likeness' (2 Cor. 3:18); 'The glory of Christ who is the likeness of God' (2 Cor. 4:4). The true image of God is seen in Christ, who – as a mirror reflects an image if in right relationship to its object – reflects God's glory. To be 'in the image of God', then, is not primarily a matter of our capacity to do anything. It is a matter of the relationship to himself which God confers on us. It is not our addressability; it is to be addressed as *Thou* by the divine *I*.

If we want to see God's image in its perfection we see it in Christ. What we see in one another is a bad reflection which, however, by a process of regeneration and resurrection can gradually be transformed. The image of God is thus both a status and a goal, a gift and a task.

Of course there are certain ontological features, certain capacities and abilities, which are involved in the *full expression* of the image of God within this world. But the point is that all of us are called to engage in the process of becoming more fully and truly human. All of us are called to grow and mature nearer to the image of God we see in Christ. And all of us are at a certain stage in that process of change.

It is entirely consistent, therefore, to believe that there is already a faint reflection, that God has already started on his work of creating a replica, at the earliest beginnings of embryonic life. Of course, the early embryo cannot be anything like a full manifestation of the divine image, but then neither can the fetus, the newborn, nor most of us sinful adults either. There is nothing inconsistent in agreeing with Richard Higginson's statement: 'Early embryos do not differ qualitatively from the rest of us; they are simply at an earlier stage of the development process. God has a history and a relationship with them too.'[3]

The second point arising from the doctrine of the *imago Dei* strengthens this view of the status of the human embryo. What discriminates between the relationship God has with trees and giraffes and the relationship he has with us, seems to be related to species identity. Out of the whole range of creatureliness God said, 'Let us make man – male and female – in our image.' It is of *this* species, and not another, that God says the members of it

---

3. Unpublished paper. *Cf.* R. Higginson, *Reply to Warnock*, Grove Books, Nottingham, 1986.

bear his image, just as it is human flesh which the divine word became in the mystery of the incarnation.

There is, therefore, a moral significance attached to being a member of the human species, which is not shared by other species. Some secular philosophers dub this 'speciesism', and find it as reprehensible as sexism or racism. But the Christian is obliged to make this fundamental discrimination. We have been addressed by God, and as it were commanded forth from the whole range of creatures to be distinct in the sense that our whole identity, what it means to be human, is bound up with our calling before God, and with the joy and responsibility of reflecting his glory. This is not something necessarily empirically observable; it is a status that is conferred on us, a responsibility that is required of us.

Now, if it is species membership rather than any capacity or ability inherent in individual members of the species that is the significant theological feature of our humanness; if, in other words, all living human beings whatever their stage of development are 'in the divine image' in the sense of being set in a relationship with God and having a history and destiny under God, then every living human being confronts me with a moral claim. In New Testament terms, every living human being is my neighbour, with a claim on me to neighbour-love. A human being does not become a nearer neighbour because he or she can do certain things, or because he or she has reached a higher stage of biological development, nor less of a neighbour because he or she lacks certain capacities. Every living human being comes under the protection of God's blessing to Noah, the covenant made with every living creature, and thus has a *prima facie* right not to be deliberately killed.

Furthermore, the heart of the meaning of neighbour-love is that my neighbour may never be treated as a means only, to however good an end; he or she must always be treated also as an end in themselves. No human being is merely someone's property to be used as an instrument for some other end. Each living human being, however young, is a partner in the human family, constituted by the divine image, and stands morally before me as my neighbour.

Psalm 139

We can now fill out these general theological reflections by referring to certain Old Testament passages which more specifically back them up, in particular Psalm 139. This psalm is often quoted in discussion about the significance of embryonic life. We do well to look at it in some detail. It is first and foremost about God – his omnipresence, his omnipotence, and his omnificence. The psalmist is struggling with these themes in the light of his own experience of God, in which he sees his whole life embedded. He is not making objective statements about God to others, he is addressing God in prayer and worship in an I-Thou relationship.

vv. 1-6 As the poet looks back over his life (vv. 1-4) he sees it beneath the searching eye of God. No matter where he is, God knows him. The astonishing fact is that in all his ways he is involved in a relationship with God hidden from the natural eye. He realises that he does not belong entirely to himself, but his life everywhere points to 'those invisible bonds which unite him to the reality of God'.[4] The human 'I' is the object of God's knowledge. To be an 'I' is to be known by God. So in v. 6 the psalmist expresses his inability to grasp God's knowledge of him.

vv. 7-12 The poet now explores ways in which he might escape from God's presence. He sets up hypothetical situations, yet explores them within the faith that it is God's spirit who is present with him. This is not the fleeing of a guilty conscience, rather the innate reaction of a man who trembles at the greatness of God. In our technological age, we need constantly to be reminded of such awe in the presence of the Almighty.

vv. 13-16 Instead of letting his mind dwell on ways of escape, the poet now turns to God in a more positive way. He understands himself in relation to this deep mystery of God's ever-presence by recalling God's creative power, and by applying this to himself. It is because God has created me that he knows me. The psalmist now understands his own existence as falling within the mystery of God's creative power. We notice in particular how these verses speak of 'my unformed substance' (the word *golen* is used only here in the Old Testament; Brown,

---

4. A.Weiser, *The Psalms*, London, 1962.

Driver and Briggs in their Hebrew lexicon translate it 'embryo').

The 'I' who is known by God is the 'I' God knit together in the womb. The 'I' who offers praise (v. 14) shares the same history under God as the 'I' who was being made in secret (v. 17). The poet is no longer overwhelmed by the magnitude of God: his own history has a place within God's providence. Most significantly of all, there is a historical continuity of personal identity affirmed here from the embryo to the mature poet.

Other Old Testament Passages

Some other paragraphs from the Old Testament strengthen this view. In Psalm 51:5, for example, David pushes the historical continuity of his life right back to conception. And Job 10:8-11 reads: 'Thy hands fashioned me and made me . . . remember that thou hast made me of clay . . . . Didst thou not pour me out like milk and curdle me like cheese?' The analogy of poured-out milk that curdles like cheese is used to illustrate the pouring out of milky seminal fluid into the female, and the development of a firm embryonic body following insemination. For a culture that knew nothing of sperm and ova this is a remarkable picture. It is also of interest that the writer does not trace the process back to the will of father and mother. Rather, 'didst *thou* not pour me out?'

Some Old Testament passages seem to indicate an opposing viewpoint. It is sometimes said, for example, that Jer. 1:4 ('Before I formed you in the womb I knew you') indicates a separation between personal life and biological life which implies that not all biological life is necessarily 'known by God' to be personal. However, Jeremiah is speaking of divine foreknowledge outside the line of personal history in time. We cannot read personal pre-existence into Jeremiah 1:4. What we can do is see in it a pointer to the divine significance accorded to Jeremiah from his very beginnings in the womb because even from before that time there was a divine destiny in mind for him.

Another problem paragraph is Exodus 21:22-5. This is part of the case law regulating the life of the desert community, the law relating to bodily injuries. Some people read this as suggesting that if there is a brawl and as a result a pregnant woman has a miscarriage but is otherwise not harmed, then a fine shall be paid, but if she is hurt, then a more severe punishment is needed. They argue from this that the life of the mother is therefore more valuable than that of the fetus.

Others follow the Septuagint translation of this verse in drawing a distinction between an 'unformed' fetus (the death of which was not to be treated as homicide) and a 'formed' fetus for which life was to be given for life. The relevance of this to deliberate actions against the life of the fetus is not clear, however, because commentators are agreed that all injury referred to in this verse is accidental. Furthermore, there may well be a better reading (followed by U. Cassuto and others[5]): 'If the woman is hurt and so gives birth prematurely, but neither the woman or the child/children die, then a fine is appropriate; but if death follows (*i.e.* of either the mother or the child/children), then you shall give life for life . . . .' It is unclear what weight should be placed on this passage. In no case does it teach that fetal life may be destroyed by choice.

Generalising from Psalm 139

We return now to Psalm 139, and to the theological significance of the poet's affirmation of a continuity of his personal identity from his adult life back to the time of his conception. This is, it might well be pointed out, the history line of a mature adult which he can trace back to his personal beginnings. Because of this some writers reject the suggestion that from this psalm we can draw general conclusions concerning the personal identity of every other human conceptus. Thus, in his article 'The Beginnings of Personal Life'[6] Donald MacKay makes a distinction between those fertilised ova which are spontaneously aborted 'at too early a stage for any of the minimal structures for recognisably personal life (not just human life) to have developed'. He calls these X's. Those that develop into normal infants and eventually adults, he calls N's. Among the N's he finds the writer of Psalm 139. 'But', says MacKay, 'Where, O where, does Psalm 139 say anything whatever about the X's of this world?' He goes on:

5. U. Cassuto, *A Commentary on the Book of Genesis*, Part 1, ET, Jerusalem, 1961.
6. Donald MacKay, *Journal of the Christian Medical Fellowship*, Volume 30:2, April 1984.

People seem to be arguing that because in Case N (where the evidence comes from those who have 'made it' as persons), God's concern for their whole world line was personal, therefore in Case X God must view the fertilised egg as a person (with the rights of a person). I don't know any canons of logic by which this follows! In the case of the N's, of course, there is direct continuity of personal identity. But in the case of the X's, on what grounds could it be claimed that there ever was a person with personal identity?

He continues later:

> In the case of the X's, then, it seems entirely consistent with the biblical data to take the view that there never has been a person there: that in this case the 'person' is only a might-have-been, and not an existent to whom moral obligations are owed.

Now, MacKay's distinction between X's and N's is made on the basis of physical structures which have or have not developed. He supports the view that the maturing nervous system goes through a sequence of stages in which qualitatively new modes of co-operative activity arise, some of which are known in later life to be essential for the maintenance of conscious personal agency,

> so that even complete continuity of biological development would not rule out the possibility of a decisive moment, or at least a decisive stage, before which there is nobody there but after which there is someone who is 'he' or 'she' as a personal cognitive agent, however limited in capacities.

Now of course there are real differences in the cognitive and agency capacities between a fertilised egg and a more developed fetus. And if one accepts that personhood is defined in terms of capacities, and that only personal entities which have a sufficient level of cognitive capacity have rights of protection, then MacKay's argument is valid. If, however, as we have argued, it is species identity that in itself constitutes a moral claim, and if the moral status of a human entity is not defined in terms of its capacities but rather in terms of God's relationship to it, then MacKay's distinction between X's and N's needs to be questioned.

From the theological perspective which I outlined earlier, it seems clear that personhood – being in the divine image – needs to be understood relationally and teleologically, and not primarily ontologically. There are, to be sure, a whole series of discontinuities in the development from an embryo to an adult. On what *theological* grounds does MacKay single out cognitive capacity as the one significant discontinuity? From the earliest moments of life right through to death, the human organism is performing metabolic functions which characterise an organic whole. Through all the various discontinuities of development, there is this continuity of organic integration which marks the continuing identity of the conceptus, embryo, fetus, child and adult.

If Professor MacKay's distinction between X's and N's is not valid, what generalised conclusions may be drawn from, for example, Psalm 139? First, the poetic power of the psalms depends on the generalisations which we make. We are involved in the psalms. Their words stand as testimonies very often not just to the truth about one individual, but about human life before God. The Lord is *my* Shepherd, not just David's. He keeps *my* going out and coming in, not just that of the author of Psalm 121. And, O Lord, thou has searched *me* and known *me*.

Secondly, and to put the argument at its weakest: even if we have to be agnostic about the appropriateness of calling every early conceptus a 'person' (and is not the destiny of naturally aborted fetuses God's question and not ours?), Psalm 139 makes clear that in some cases at least (such as this psalmist) there is a continuity of personal identity from conception to maturity. Given what we are clearly told about such cases, and the fact that we are not told anything at all about the others, we ought to steer well clear of utterly unjustifiably treating the cases we are not told about in an entirely opposite way from those in relevantly similar circumstances of which we have some knowledge. If the personal 'I' of this poet in embryo is an innocent human being with an inviolable right to life, we should beware of presuming to know that other embryonic life is definitely not. And in any case, *we* are not, of course, in a position to know which embryos will have an on-going personal history, and which will not.

There are a number of features of the opening chapters of the Gospels, particularly Luke, and the doctrine of the incarnation which they imply, which cast some further light on the status of the human embryo.

The Virginal Conception of Jesus

As T. F. Torrance[7] and others have argued, indeed the seeds are present in Calvin, one of the crucially significant corollaries to be found in the doctrine of the virginal conception of Jesus is that the divine Son of God has joined himself with human flesh precisely at the point of conception. The Word has become flesh, so to speak, right down to the level of our genes. In his role as Mediator, Christ has taken our humanity, our human flesh from conception onwards, into relationship with God in a decisively new way. This confers on the human embryo a sacred and inviolable status. 'The Lord Jesus assumed our human nature, gathering up all its stages and healing them in his own human life, including conception.'[8] There is a human continuity through all these stages from conceptus to mature adult.

Brephos – There are two sets of biblical texts which support this line of argument. The first is the continuity implied by the use of the Greek *brephos,* particularly by St Luke. In classical usage, *brephos* can mean both 'embryo' and 'child'. There is a passage in Homer (Il .23.266) which talks about some games in which the first prize offered is 'a woman with a tripod', and the second prize is of a 'mare pregnant with the brephos of a mule'. The lexicons translate *brephos* in this instance 'embryo'. In St Luke the references are all human, but there is a variety of contexts. In 1:41 the 'babe' leaped in Elizabeth's womb on hearing Mary's news; in 2:12,16 Luke writes of a 'babe' lying in a manger. In Luke 18:25: 'Now they were bringing infants to him that he might touch them' (*cf.* Acts 7:19). Some sort of continuity is implied linking embryo, child in the womb, newborn baby, and infant.

The visitation – The other support comes from the narrative of Mary's visit to Elizabeth recorded in Luke 1.39f. Within at most a few days after the Angel's visit to Mary, she was on the road. Elizabeth's house could not have been more than ten days' donkey ride away, so it is the natural reading of this pas-

---

7. *Test Tube Babies*, Edinburgh, 1984.
8. T. F. Torrance, *Op cit.*, p. 10.

sage that Mary arrives at Elizabeth's house with a ten day old fetus (to be called Jesus when he is born) in her womb. The greeting by Elizabeth is full of significance: she calls Mary 'the mother of my Lord'. Elizabeth recognises Mary as already a mother, even though the fetus in her womb was no bigger than a pin-head. And then the fetal Messiah is recognised by the six-month old fetus, the still-to-be-born John the Baptist, jumping with joy in Elizabeth's womb!

Thus the American Benedictine Stanley Jaki comments:

> A lucky John, whom our Supreme Court (though not the widespread medical practice) would have protected. As to the Messiah, only a two-week old fetus, he would not have been granted any protection by that august Court.

Parenthood

Taking our cue from Elizabeth's greeting to Mary, we may suggest that, rather than asking 'When does human life begin?', a more biblical way of posing the question might well be, 'When does parenthood begin?' What is the significance of parenthood under God?

The creation story implies that procreation is a divine command ('Be fruitful and multiply'); and the psalmist tells us that children are a blessing (*cf.* Ps. 127:5). Now let us put these themes alongside two other biblical paragraphs. At the opening of the Gospel of John, we read of God's creative Word that 'all things were made through him, and without him was not anything made that was made'. And in Ephesians 5, the love relationship between husband and wife is to be patterned on the love relationship which that same God in Christ has with his church. Because of our view of the unity of God, we can thus see that within the Godhead love and creativity belong together, and so the human procreative process in which love and creativity normatively (although, of course, not always in practice) belong together is a sharing in the loving creativity of God through whom all things were made.

The child conceived is thus begotten through the human relationship, though brought into being by God. As such he or she is to be welcomed as a neighbour within the human family. His or her life is a gift of God's love. Parents do not, then, 'make' children as products; they share in God's creativity by begetting.

As another psalmist has put it: 'It is he that has made us and not we ourselves' (Ps.100:3).

This view is supported by the notion that conception is a 'gift' (*cf.* Ruth 4:13: 'the Lord gave conception'; *cf.* also Gen. 1:25; 21:1,2: 25:21; 29:31-35; 30:17-24; 33:5; Dt. 7:13; Jud. 13:2-7; 1 Sam. 1:1-20; Ps. 113:9; 127:3-5; 128:1-6; Is. 54:1; Lk. 1:24). It is supported also by the view of some biblical writers that an 'untimely birth' expresses something unnatural, inappropriate and sometimes under divine displeasure (Ps. 58:8; Job 3:10-16; Eccles. 6:3; *cf.* 1 Cor. 15:8).

To be a parent, then (we are talking normatively, not descriptively), is to have a calling under God to share in his creative love. This must count against any view which sees the conceptus merely as a product. The conceptus, rather, must be seen and welcomed as a neighbour. A 'product' is subject to human will and human disposal; a 'neighbour' exercises a moral claim. If the 'product of conception' is in any sense a sign of God's loving creativity, then the claim it exercises on me is a claim not to be treated as a product, and so as a means only, but as a neighbour, and so as an end also.

I do not believe that to insist that the loving and procreative aspects of human sexual relationship belong normatively together rules out all contraception. But it is an altogether different question, when faced with the fact that one *has become* a parent, whether the rejection of that life can be compatible with the nature of God in whom love and creativity are joined, and before whom parenthood has the status of a calling.

'Souls'

Finally, the argument is sometimes heard that God is not really concerned with biological life at all, but rather with our 'souls', and that it is by no means clear that the 'soul' is 'added' at fertilisation. This sort of language misunderstands the Hebraic ways of speaking of human beings. You do not 'have' a soul, in a sense you are a soul; likewise you do not 'have' a body, in a different sense you are a body. The various aspects to our make-up (heart, soul, body, flesh, spirit) are ways of speaking of the whole of us. Essentially we are psychophysical unities, embodied souls and ensouled bodies. There is no living human being without a body (whether a physical body, or the 'spiritual' body of resurrection). When we are in the presence of a living human body, we are in the presence of a living human being.

It is of human beings that God said they are to reflect his image. It is of innocent human beings that God says they are not to be deliberately killed. It is neighbour-love towards human beings which requires that they are not to be used as means to another end, however good.

And that, so it seems to me, includes the youngest members of the species as well as the rest of us.[9]

---

9. This paper is the transcript of a conference address.

WHAT KIND OF BEING IS THE HUMAN EMBRYO?

TERESA IGLESIAS

1. The question 'What kind of being is the human embryo?' contains two main concepts: 'kind of being' and 'human embryo'. The first concept presupposes that there are a variety of kinds of being, or entity, in reality. One kind of being is those natural entities like stones and rocks which we call non-living beings, inanimate entities. There are other non-living entities like motorcars and chairs which we describe as artifacts, and some others which we describe as works of art, such as paintings. These are entities brought about by human design and human hands; they are not products of the natural world itself.

2. Other kinds of natural entity are plants and animals, among which the human being counts as one kind of animal within the various mammalian species. Plants and animals are living beings, animate beings. In these beings what we call 'life' is manifested. The human embryo – as any other animal embryo – counts among the living beings of nature. It is not an inanimate entity, like a rock, or an artifact like a machine. I shall come to this point later; it is of great importance, although apparently obvious.

3. The concept of the 'human embryo' is referred to in a variety of ways in current biomedical literature and in public debate. Let me mention some of these descriptions by way of illustration: 'pre-embryo' (quite recently coined), 'cluster of cells', 'a human biological node', 'human embryonic material', 'a biological being', 'not a full human', 'a potential human', 'a full human', 'a human being', 'a human personal being', 'a blob of cells', 'the product of conception', 'a conceptus'. What is behind this variety of descriptions – some of them incompatible with others – of one and the same being? It is the question of the true *ontological status,* of the human embryo, *i.e.* the question concerning the specific kind of being the human embryo is. By 'human embryo' I understand the *human conceptus,* formed when the process of fertilisation is completed, and persisting through all its subsequent stages of development before it

acquires human form. After that stage the human conceptus is usually described as a fetus until the time of birth.

The questions, then, which we have to consider are these: Is the human embryo a mere conglomeration of molecules and cells, 'human embryonic material'? Is the human embryo a living human being but not a human person? Is the embryo a living human being and a human person? My conviction is that the human embryo is a human person, a being of human nature with an eternal destiny. I take this conviction to be true, and grounded on biological knowledge, philosophical reflection and the Christian faith and way of life which I share with other Christians in the community we form as a Church. But this conviction is not universal. Hence it is my responsibility to contribute and witness to this conviction in dialogue and cooperation to the best of my ability. This is what we are here for.

4. Our attitude cannot be one of avoiding the issue of the status of the embryo altogether, either because it is difficult or because if does not suit us. People of conscience and integrity have to face difficult questions when they are important. In June 1985 the Board for Social Responsibility of the Church of England issued a Report on Human Fertilisation and Embryology entitled *Personal Origins*. On page 33, section 97 of this report we read:

> However difficult it may be to decide whether the early embryo is, or is not, a human being, in the most important sense of the term, the question to be resolved is still whether something is or is not the case, and not some other kind of question.

In this particular context 'whether something is or is not the case' means whether the human embryo is a human being in the full sense or not, *i.e.* whether it is or is not one of us, a being of full humanity and personal life. The real question indeed is one of 'to be or not to be'. It is an ontological question, a question connected with 'being'. The text of *Personal Origins* continues:

> Some of our contemporaries have hoped to avoid the question of the embryo's status altogether, and have thought it possible to move directly to a purely deliberative question: how are we to *act* towards the early embryo? The implication of this manoeuvre would seem to be that human status is not so much discerned as conferred; that social practice is sufficient of itself to validate the claims of any pretence to humanity.

The authors of this report . . . are agreed in finding this solution unsatisfactory.

5. So do I. For it is clear that if I do not know what kind of being the human embryo is, neither will I know how I should act towards it. If I do not know for certain what the human embryo really is, then I cannot know what is its proper value and hence the moral claims it has upon me. It is clear that we need to know what things are as a necessary condition for knowing how we should treat them and the kind of respect owing to them.

Questions of 'being' and 'not being' are not a mere matter of human decision. Rather, they require a sense of human and intellectual responsibility in the recognition and appreciation of what is true independently of our wishes. An attitude of respect for truth, the whole truth, is the necessary presupposition for determining questions of 'what is' and 'what is not' making possible the advancement of true wisdom and knowledge. Michael Polanyi has written in connection with this attitude:

> A man who has learned to respect the truth will feel entitled to uphold the truth against the very society which has taught him to respect it. He will indeed demand respect for himself on the grounds of his own respect for truth, and this will be accepted, even against their own inclinations, by those who share his basic convictions. Such is the equality of men in a free society.[1]

6. The majority of the signatories of the Warnock Report are to be included among those of our contemporaries referred to in *Personal Origins* who have avoided the crucial matter of the ontological status of the human embryo, namely: whether it is or is not a human person. The Report states:

> Although the questions of when life or personhood begin appear to be questions of fact susceptible of straightforward answers, we hold that the answers to such questions in fact are complex amalgams of factual and moral judgements. Instead of trying to answer these questions directly we have therefore gone straight to the question of *how it is right to treat the human embryo*. We have considered what status ought to be accorded to the human embryo, and the answer we give must necessarily be in terms of ethical or moral principles. (11.9)

---

1. *The Study of Man*, Chicago, 1985, pp. 61-62.

7. The question 'How is it right to treat the human embryo?' has been answered in the Warnock Report in two ways. The right way to treat *some* human embryos is to consider them as mere means for the benefit of other human beings; some human embryos can be bought and sold, possessed and treated as property, harmed, destroyed and disposed of; some human embryos can be generated for the sole purpose of experimentation and then disposed of before day 14. Of course, not all human embryos should be treated this way, for then there would not be test-tube babies, nor indeed babies at all; it would clearly be the end of the human species. Why only *some* should be treated in this way and not others, and which ones are in what group, is really a matter of chance determined by the intentions and interests of the generators.

The second answer found in the Warnock Report as to how it is right to treat the human embryo is given in Dissent Form B signed by Madeline Carriline, John Marshall, and Jean Walker. It is broadly this (although some qualifications would be needed): *Every human embryo* should be generated with the sole purpose of allowing it to live and develop following its normal course of development; human embryos are not to be deliberately used, harmed and destroyed as mere instruments for the benefit of others; they are not to be generated with a view to their destruction in order to improve the results of *in vitro* fertilisation or the advance of knowledge.

8. The moral principles in the light of which these two different answers are given are not explicitly stated in the Report but they are clearly discernible. The principles are based on the two alternative basic evaluations of the individual human being.

(a) The individual human being is of no intrinsic worth, he may be deliberately exploited or harmed or destroyed for the benefits of others. He is of instrumental value; he need not be respected and treated as an end in itself.

(b) The individual human being is of intrinsic worth, he cannot deliberately be used, exploited, harmed or destroyed for the benefits of others. He is of non-instrumental value; he must be respected and treated as an end and not as a mere means.

The signatories of the majority report profess to accept the general moral principle that the human being is an end in itself and should never be exploited by another human being in the case of *e.g.* human adults, but they qualify their acceptance of the principle by saying that it applies 'in almost every case'.

The Report states:

> Even in compelling medical circumstances the danger of exploitation of one human being by another appears to the majority of us far to outweigh the potential benefits, in almost every case. That people should treat others as means to their own ends, however desirable the consequences must always be liable to moral objection. (8.17)

It would be no good to me or you if, in the implementation of this principle, we happened to be the exceptional cases not included in 'almost every case'.

9. The signatories of the Report cannot avoid adopting a position about the kind of being the human embryo is, and here they are all of one accord: the human embryo is *a potential human being*, or a potential human person (see 11.22 and Dissent Form B.3). By this is meant that the human embryo is the kind of being that of itself, given nurture, will develop to a stage at which every one will recognise it to be a human person. Put in more simple terms, whether we like it or not, you and I and the signatories of the Warnock Report have to recognise that we have been human embryos, human beings of embryonic form. There is no way in which we can deny this truth.

10. Yet the *moral significance* that the committee members recognise in this potential differs. For the majority of them it is not of much significance at all: the early embryo can be treated as a chattel. In contrast Carriline, Marshall and Walker recognise that a being that is regarded as a potential human has a special status in virtue of this *potential*. They put it: 'It is in our view wrong to create something with the potential for becoming a human person and then deliberately destroy it.'

They give an illuminating medical analogy to support their view: 'at no stage was a transplant undertaken with the intention the patient should not survive.'

11. Let me stress the fundamental point I want to make in what I have said. Underlying current medico-scientific trends which support experimentation on human embryos at the ex-

pense of their integrity and well-being, there is a valuation of the individual human being which rests on two basic presuppositions: the first has to do with morality while the second is an ontological presupposition.

(i) The value and interests of science and the rest of society *may override* the value and interests of the individual human being; the human being is of instrumental value.

(ii) The newly-conceived human, the human embryo, does not enjoy full human status like one of us, for it is not a human being or a human person, but only a potential one.

Clearly, for those who hold that the human being is of no intrinsic worth, whether the human embryo is a full human or not is of no importance. For even if it were a human being, given pressing needs, it could be deliberately harmed or 'sacrificed' for the benefit of others as a child or adult might be. If innocent human beings can be harmed, killed, 'sacrificed' for others, the human embryo obviously can. To uphold this view that the innocent human being can be deliberately exploited, harmed and destroyed is to abolish the basis on which all legal and natural justice rests. If large numbers in our society advocate or practically live by this view and attitude it is an indication of the enormous need for true moral witness and effort to counteract that trend. Let us recall that slavery was declared illegal in Britain in 1807 after the bill for its abolition had been introduced in the House of Commons, debated and defeated eleven times.

12. Let me now focus on the second presupposition mentioned above, namely that the human embryo is only a potential human person, and that therefore to harm or destroy it is not to destroy a human person.

Current embryological knowledge about the generation of animals and human beings clearly establishes the fact that every conceptus begins once the process of fertilisation has been completed. We all know that the new human conceptus will grow of itself into the adult being. Why is it, then, that many of our contemporaries do not recognise in this very fact that we all share a common humanity, and that as humanly equal we should all equally be respected? Why is it that the *same embryological facts* are interpreted and accorded a different significance? Why is it so difficult for many to recognise that the terms 'human being' and 'human person' are *absolute* terms, *i.e.* that a living human being is either one or the other and that you cannot have 'half a human being', 'half a human person', just as you can't have 'half a dog', but you may have 'half a house' *progressively* becoming one? Our problems do not lie with what embryology books clearly describe. Where do they lie?

13. They may lie with a defective attitude of lack of respect for the whole truth – as pointed out earlier – but clearly this is not always the case. Some would put it this way: 'Yes, we know we begin as organic beings at conception, but the issue is not whether the human embryo is a human being or not – for it is one – but whether it is a human person.' The question is not: 'When does a member of the human species come into existence?' but rather 'When does a human person come into existence?' The problem, then, is not a matter of biology or embryology, so what is the nature of the problem?

14. Most of the fundamental problems of life are concerned with general attitudes of mind, with outlooks, with overall frameworks or points of view, more than with mere matters of detail. So it is possible that a limited outlook may not permit us to appreciate the true significance of the embryological facts and so understand the kind of *biological beings* we are; it may also prevent us from seeing the kind of *personal beings* we are. Let me draw your attention to two of these outlooks or frameworks which act like 'mental glasses' through which reality is viewed. They are deeply engrained in our society and underlie current evaluations of the whole of living reality in general and of the human conceptus in particular. One of these frameworks has been described as 'mechanistic Darwinism' and the other as 'Cartesian dualism'; both are closely related.[2]

15. *Mechanistic Darwinism* is a form of 'scientism'. It is an outlook shared by many scientists and non-scientists. In this outlook the living being is regarded ultimately as nothing more than a very perfect machine. In fact there are no living beings, but only inanimate reality. The living being is ultimately a well

---

2. For a discussion of the first see David Holbrook, 'Medical Ethics and the Potentialities of the Living Being', *British Medical Journal*, 291, 17 August 1985, pp. 459-62.

organised conglomeration of molecules or a mass of cells. Molecules constitute the ultimate ingredients of life, its essence. They pass from generation to generation in a continuous chain; thus, life has no specific beginning or end, but it is a process: 'nature is only a self-perpetuating machine'. In this perspective to call an entity unique means simply to say that it is a combinatorial reassortment of molecules; this is the case with any living conceptus, as it is also the case therefore with any mature ovum and sperm. Thus, the *potentialities* of living beings do not radically differ in nature from those of non-living entities and artifacts. A scientist involved in IVF, H. Jones (1982) has stated this point thus:

> It is sometimes said that the embryo if not a human person is potentially a human person, and therefore should be treated as such. But in this sense, so is the egg or the sperm. A chassis with four wheels attached to the beginning of the assembly line is potentially an automobile, but no-one would buy it for such until it was developed into an object which could be driven away from the line. At the beginning, it is potentially an automobile, just as is the iron from the mountain.[3]

If 'life' is ultimately denied, and explained by mechanistic laws, and if the living being is reduced to combination, replications and synthesis of molecules, how can the human embryo be understood? If after all life is chemistry, the questions of morality and philosophy are non-questions, and whatever the true questions are, molecular physics and chemistry will provide the answers to them. Science will finally tell us what 'life' and 'persons' are. There is no realm of reality beyond the realm of scientific observation.

16. The biological and philosophical significance and implications of recognising 'biological entities' as *living beings,* as *organic living wholes,* must be appreciated against the mechanistic outlook, if the nature of our embryonic and adult being is to be appreciated. So let me dwell for a moment on the truth that a living being is a living organic whole, with living autonomy, dynamic organisation and potentiality.

17. The living being is generated as a whole, it develops and sustains itself as a whole, and it dies as a whole. The living or-

---

3. *Human Conception in vitro* R.G. Edwards & J. Purdy, Eds., London, 1982, p. 54.

ganism manifests itself to be a whole by its unified organic constitution and powers of self-growth, self-organisation, self-preservation, self-fulfilment, even self-healing. We indeed observe the living organism to come into being as a living whole, to move and function as a whole, to grow as a whole, to die as a whole. These characteristics cannot be attributed, for example, to 'the brain as a whole'; that is why the brain is not identical with the 'organism as a whole' but is rather one of the organism's vital parts or organs. The unity of the living whole does not reside in any of its parts, because that unity is *not caused* by any one of its parts: the brain does not cause the unity of the living human organism, nor of any other vital organ or system. If the brain were the source and cause of the unity of the living organism it would have primacy over other parts of the whole, *e.g.* it would be the *germinal* whole itself and the first generated so that it could cause the unity of all the other parts and their organisation. This is obviously not the case. The true primacy is that of the whole, of the living unit and its organisation: it is an ontological primacy over all the parts either considered singly or as a totality. The brain and all the other parts or organs develop in harmony with each other manifesting at every stage the unified organic activity of the whole. The unity and power of the whole determines – and is prior to – the form and function of the parts. The whole produces all its parts for self-maintenance at every stage of its existence, tending towards its own self-maturity. Given appropriate protection and nourishment the organic whole takes care of itself. Any part of the organism, any vital organ be it brain, heart, lung, kidneys, liver, *etc.*, are so related to each other, and to all the other parts and systems of the organism, that none of them can be regarded singly as a 'biologically independent unit' – or as causing that unity: the organism as a whole must be regarded as that unity by its own organic constitution and self-sustaining powers.

18. To claim that the unity or wholeness of the organism is not caused by any of its parts, and that nor does it reside in any of its parts, is not equivalent to claiming that the destruction of any part does not cause the destruction or death of the organism as a whole. Although a living unit is not caused by any one of its elements its destruction may be brought about by the de-

struction of one of those elements. Clearly, the death of the brain, or of the heart or the lungs, causes the death of the whole.

19. That living beings are not considered living wholes by some scientists can be illustrated by some comments of Sir Andrew Huxley, President of the Royal Society and Nobel Prize Winner in Physiology. He considers that there is an ambiguity in the use of the term 'embryo'. He wrote in the *New Scientist*[4] – and note the terminology he uses:

> The ambiguity arises because the word 'embryo' is also used to denote the *whole of the collection of cells* formed by repeated division of the fertilised egg during the first two weeks or so, although only a few per cent of these cells are destined to become the embryo proper, by far the greater number of them will turn into extra-embryonic tissue and ultimately into the structures that are discarded as the afterbirth. Furthermore, it is indeterminate which particular cells will form the embryo proper.
>
> The embryo proper is first recognisable at about 15th day after fertilisation when a specialised region of cells called the 'primitive streak' first appears. Before that stage, it cannot be said that a definitive embryo exists: *the product of conception is a structure* of which a small and undetermined part will – if development proceeds normally – form a 'primitive streak' and later an 'embryo' in the sense in which the word is generally understood, and later again a 'fetus'.

'The product of conception is a structure.' Is it not a living being? Is the being generated as a whole at the 15th day? Are not the 'afterbirth', *i.e.* placenta and membranes, much needed organic parts of the whole being which are developed for its sustenance as other parts are? Can the word 'pre-embryo', coined to abolish the alleged ambiguity mentioned by Sir Andrew Huxley, prevent the early embryo from being a living being generated and growing as a whole during the previous 14 days when it was a 'pre-embryo'? 'Cosmetic semantics' cannot change the nature of reality.

20. *Cartesian Dualism.* Those who espouse a form of scientism similar to that of Sir Andrew Huxley believe that 'the collection of cells formed by repeated divisions of the fertilised egg' is first merely 'a collection of cells', and that then, by the 14th day, something happens, so that what was before a non-

---

4. 11 April 1985, p.2, italics mine.

living being becomes a living being, the 'individual', the whole.

A similar position is maintained by those who espouse a radical dualism of a Cartesian form. In radical dualism the belief is that we are constituted by a living body (or a 'biological being') and a soul, and that at some stage the two entities may exist separately and then come together. Thus, a question for dualists is this: at what point in the development of the human organism (or the human being) does the spiritual soul enter the body? For to be a person is to possess an immortal soul, and as the evangelical geneticist Professor R.J. Berry has stated: 'It is a false extrapolation to assume that the "life" from God which transforms a biological being into a spiritual one is automatically given to every fertilised egg.'[5] A Catholic theologian John Mahoney in his book *Bioethics and Belief*[6] states the matter thus: '. . .it may be possible to have a human being which has not yet received a human soul infused by God and is therefore not yet a human person'. Professor Berry calls the human being only a 'biological being' and Fr Mahoney 'a human biological node'.

21. Note one of the assumptions on which this position rests. It is possible to have a living being of the human kind, a member of the human species – a human being – and yet not to have a human person. What kind of *metaphysical* being is that? No account of it is given. Let me mention in brief that for true Aristotelianism the soul is the form of the body; the soul is the principle of life; hence by definition, to be a living human being is to possess a human soul; you could not be a being of the *human kind* and not possess a soul.

22. How is it possible to know when the soul comes into a living human being and goes out of him? What criteria would count as valid? 'None', it would be claimed, for the soul cannot be observed or scientifically detected. Hence it is argued that as we cannot know at what point the soul comes into the body or goes out of it, we cannot know when a person begins to exist or dies. We must remain agnostic in this matter. But must we?

All the potentialities which one needs if one is to acquire the mental and spiritual activities of the human person are inextrica-

---

5. *The Times*, February 6 1980, col.6, p. 15.
6. London, 1984, p. 69.

bly bound up with the embryo's potential to develop all organs including the brain; in this sense the human conceptus is 'organically complete', nothing can be added to it. Why then is it that the human conceptus is not 'personally complete'? If *all* potential is *actually present* in the conceptus why has it not a soul? What are the *reasons* or 'indicators' which suggest that the human conceptus is not a personal being and has not a soul? John Mahoney summarises the opinion of many in this matter when he says: 'the possibility of twinning and recombination in every conceptus (whether it occurs spontaneously or not) argues against a biologically stable subject for such immediate animation.'[7] Thus, the fundamental reasons why we may doubt that the human conceptus is a human person are ultimately founded on *empirical facts* which put the 'philosophical and theological doctrine of the human soul . . . in a thoroughly unsatisfactory state.'[8] Let me consider first the biological facts of twinning and recombination and then talk about the doctrine of the soul.

23. The picture we are given of twinning and recombination in public debate is constructed through the glasses of 'mechanism' as described above. The general picture we are given is that the early embryo is a conglomeration of 'undifferentiated' cells. So the embryo in these early days can enter or be brought into subsequent divisions and aggregations of various kinds, and when these divisions, combinations or aggregations can no longer be carried out we have a stable individual, no longer capable of becoming two (or more) or of fusing with another living being. It is only at that stage that the 'splitting' of the soul cannot occur, because only then do we have a 'stable' individual, not before. Let me dwell for a moment on the misleading scientific picture which underlies this view.

24. *First,* the organic mechanisms of natural monozygotic twinnings are not yet fully understood and known; there are good indications for believing that they are genetically determined and hence that the two beings emerge as *two* from conception, but even if this was found out not to be the case on empirical grounds, there are no empirical grounds either for main-

7. *Ibid.,* p. 81.
8. *Ibid.,* p. 100.

taining that a living being as a whole 'splits' into two new living beings – as discussed below. *Second,* recombination of full embryos to form a single chimeric one has not been proved to occur naturally, either in humans or in any other mammalian species. *Third,* the early embryo is not an undifferentiated being, either molecularly, cellularly or morphologically; it is of the human species and genetically unique; molecular differentiating activity in the cells of the conceptus (both intra-cellular and inter-cellular) is present from its beginning leading to its full differentiation and formation. Visible differentiation of cells only reflects the emerging differences in their protein and enzyme content; the code for all proteins is spelled out by genetic messages reaching the cytoplasm from the nucleus. This molecular activity between nucleus and cytoplasm is species-specific in the conceptus and active from its very beginning, embryologists tell us; organically the embryo 'knows' where it is going. The law of its *organic finality* is dynamically written within itself at every stage of its existence from the moment it is formed as a conceptus when fertilisation is completed. *Fourth,* it is indeed a fact that the cells of the very early embryo can be disaggregated, aggregated, recombined to form chimeric embryos in laboratory conditions (the 'geep' – a chimera of sheep and goat produced in Cambridge is a good illustration). This fact manifests the regulatory capacity and powers that the early embryonic beings possess in order:

(i) to make themselves whole again when some substantial part of the organism has been removed or damaged

(ii) to assimilate or integrate into their organic wholeness molecular, cellular or organ parts from other organisms. In other words powers of 'grafting', 'transplant', 'healing', 'regeneration', are present in the early living embryonic being.

25. This is the most important point as regards aggregation and disaggregation of the early embryos of higher animals. Organically, because living beings are wholes constituted of parts (organs), they can be manipulated, they can be literally 'mixed up'; yet, *this mixing up is not of living being as wholes or of whole living beings but of their parts.* Let me give you an example. If one cell of a four-cell sheep embryo is separated from the others and allowed to develop on its own, it may give rise to

a whole sheep, and so will the other original three cells. The individual cell, once separated, is a *fragment* which now becomes a whole itself. But before the separation the cell was only part of a whole. Thus because a *part* of a being has the capacity to become a whole if separated from it, it does not cease to be a part when it is playing its own function within the whole. This general idea may be expressed in the following four propositions:

> a. Living beings are organic wholes; as such they can shed parts (cells) which may become parts of other organisms.
> b. Living beings can shed parts (cells) which may become new organic wholes themselves, either on their own or in combination with others.
> c. Living beings can be deprived of or damaged in substantial organic parts and yet regulate or regenerate themselves to continue to develop as well-functioning wholes.
> d. Living beings (of mammalian species) as *whole beings* neither divide from nor fuse with other whole beings, but their parts which they shed can.

Thus, there is *fragmentation* of parts of living beings giving rise to asexual generation, but there is no 'fusion' and 'splitting' of living beings as *total wholes*. So if there is no fusion and splitting of beings there could not be a problem of 'splitting' of souls. Every living being is individual, *i.e.* organically individuated in all its dimensions from its generation to its death. The early embryo as a living whole is an individual stable organism.

The 'Soul' and the Truths of Faith: a Task for the Theologian

26. From a philosophical point of view, the doctrine of the soul finds its roots in Greek philosophy. Philosophical doctrines, Christians would maintain, are not truths of faith, or truths of revelation. Truths of faith are not founded on philosophical doctrine; but ultimately on the authority of God himself whom we trust. Truths of faith are not human achievements as philosophical doctrines are. For this reason the task of a theologian (and so of a moral theologian) rests on this foundation:

. . .that accepting the truth of Catholic faith present in the living Church of which one is a member, one seeks a better understanding of this truth in which one already lives.[9]

Thus, 'theology neither calls into question the truth of faith nor attempts to prove it. There is no superior standard by which to criticise or establish the word of God.'[10]

27. An important question for the theologian might be this: what truths of faith are we seeking to understand better by means of the doctrine of the soul? Truths of the faith are *living truths and attitudes* in the Christian community before they are ever formulated in principles and explained in doctrines. The divinity of Christ and the eucharist are clear examples of this. Another legitimate question that a theologian may ask is this: what truths of faith have we received concerning the *kind of beings we are?* We could point to some:

- each one of us is created by God as a personal unique being in his image;

- each one of us is called to share with God eternal life in friendship with him as a 'thou' to him;

- we are to respect one another unconditionally as children of God, and we are never to destroy a human life from conception;

- the Word of God became flesh, assumed our bodily nature and became like one of us from conception (not at the 14th day).

28. These truths cannot be changed by philosophical doctrines, even if the doctrines which once were helpful in understanding those truths are no longer so; this may be the case with the doctrine of the soul; so theologians may have to consider in what respect development of doctrine is needed. But development of doctrine cannot mean the questioning of truths of faith.

9. G. Grisez, *The Way of Lord Jesus. Christian Moral Principles*, Chicago, 1983, p. 7.
10. *Ibid.*, pp. 7-78.

A recent authoritative presentation of some of the truths mentioned above is found in the words of John Paul II quoted by the Anglican Bishop of Norwich in a recent speech in the House of Lords:

> The world has largely lost respect for human life from the moment of conception. The world is weak in upholding the indissoluble unity of marriage. It fails to support the stability and holiness of family life. There is a crisis of truth and responsibility in human relationships. And so I support with all my heart those who recognise and defend the law of God that governs human life. We must never forget that every person, from the moment of conception to the last breath, is a unique child of God and has a right to life'.[11]

29. That a human personal being begins to exist at conception is a truth now supported by our biological knowledge and philosophical insight and Christian faith. For human beings come into existence at conception with that capacity or power to become the *personal being* we all recognise in the adult. As a colleague of mine Luke Gormally has put it:

> The continuity of development of the organism has a significance of more than biological import. From a philosophical point of view continuity of development requires us to assume that the development *must be informed from the beginning* by a principle of life which is personal in nature. How otherwise can this organic development be for the sake of a mature, unified life which is personal in character?[12]

It is in and through our bodies that we are the specific kind of persons we are: our bodily constitution is the kind of personal humanity that all members of the human family share. The living human organism is the living human person. There are not stages in our existence when this identity does not hold. From conception to death every human being is a personal being in virtue of which his life, bodily integrity and conscience are always to be respected.

---

11. *Hansard*, 31 October 1984.
12. From an unpublished manuscript.

PROBLEMS RAISED BY ARTIFICIAL HUMAN REPRODUCTION

IAN DONALD

The Warnock Report is well worth reading and one is easily beguiled by its good English. The coverage is wide and clear and many of the 63 recommendations are not contentious. The description in lay terms of a very wide variety of techniques and their possible consequences can be easily read and understood by anyone. This said, one should not be deceived by its mellifluence and failure to crack down on a whole range of evils with the possible exception of commercial surrogacy.

It is a totally secular, irreligious type of report which would satisfy any atheist, and because of the sweeping possibilities of what has been called the 'reproduction revolution', Christians, in fact any who believe in the existence of God, Muslim as well as Jew, cannot fail to recognise its passive acceptance of much that is evil or potentially so.

The prophet Jeremiah described it very accurately when referring to the reaction of the Lord. 'For my people have committed two evils, they have forsaken me, the fountain of living waters and hewed them out cisterns, broken cisterns that can hold no water'. (2:13)

Having rejected, or rather not even considered, God's wonderful creation, the members of the committee unashamedly ignored matters spiritual, whatever their private convictions. In fact the Fountain of Living Waters is shut out from their utilitarian outlook.

Now let us look at the leaking cracks in the cisterns.

The tragedy of childlessness is more akin to bereavement than to an illness, nevertheless when it is something which medical science can correct, then it should be corrected. The birth of Louise Brown seven years ago was a justified triumph. Yet childlessness, though a reason for *in vitro* fertilisation, is not an excuse for much that is now being done or contemplated.

Here there are two enormous cracks in the cistern. The first employs the intrusion of a third party into the marital relationship which all Christians are committed to accepting. This may come under four main headings: (a) Donated sperm, (b) Donated ova or eggs, (c) Surrogacy and (d) Embryo transfer, nowadays by early lavage within a very few days of conception. The other huge crack opens up on the question of human experimentation.

Let us take experimentation first. The Warnock Report accepts the use of embryonic life up to 14 days under supposed licensed control, so that the human embryo can be frozen, stored, discarded, donated, dissected and generally made use of subject to a 'statutory licensing authority'. This itself is an absurdity. Its constitution (even to including a layman), its powers of assessment and enforcement would be ineffectual. It would be easily hoodwinked or bamboozled and a whole army of bureaucrats of varying degrees of ignorance would be necessary or the number of units would have to be reduced to a very select few. So human life is to be put to the service of science. Outside Hitler's Germany this has never been accepted by medicine. Talk of research being necessary to improve the rather dismal success rate of *in vitro* fertilisation is not very convincing. The fertilisation is fairly easy. It is the implantation and maintenance *in utero* that is the real problem. Experimentation does not include observation to ensure that the embryo is developing sufficiently well to be implanted into the recipient mother-to-be, nor do attempts to improve the implantation chances count as research because in such instances the interests of the embryo itself are being served

What is detestable about experimenting on humans, born or unborn, handicapped, sick or dying is where the interests of scientific advance are the object of the exercise. The excuse that abnormalities of development might be better understood and, hopefully, corrected wears a bit thin, and as for getting better understanding of cancer – this sort of talk to a frightened public verges on the dishonest. Furthermore, the deliberate cultivation of embryos to provide spare parts for a recipient, if necessary by cloning from his own nuclei in order to minimise the chances of rejection, *e.g.* kidney, liver, pancreas transplants, is the ultimate in scientific depravity.

Spare embryos are obvious targets for research and exploitation and now that the nucleus, and hence the genetic material, can be substituted, modified, altered and replicated in an infinite number of clones as is already possible in veterinary science, it puts the whole question of God's image and purpose in creation into the dustbin. The vets may indeed be interested in breeding cattle with more meat on their bones or giving higher milk yields but the Warnock belief that a statutory licensing authority could, or would control this in the human species is naive to the point of simple-mindedness. Scientists are not all saints. Just ask a survivor of Hiroshima or Nagasaki about that!

Breeding, including clone breeding to specification is indeed a threat to human life, not because of numbers but because of the cheapening and accepted expendability of human life which will be engendered in mankind's regard for his own species. It is a sort of scientific cannibalism which is envisaged, all for 'the greatest good of the greatest number'.

Very close at hand is sex selection, which because of its obvious preference for males, especially in countries where the number of children is more or less rationed, could easily upset the social order yet, while acknowledging this, the Report seems satisfied even to approve a DIY kit provided that it could be shown to be safe and reliable. Yet further off, too far in fact to be considered by the committee, is ectogenesis. In fact this could come about by the turn of the century by narrowing the gap between the longest period over which the embryo could be kept alive outside the uterus (the 14-day limit already long forgotten) and the earliest stage at which modern paediatric technology could keep an ultrapremature fetus alive. Meanwhile although the Report is opposed, rather tamely, to using a surrogate related mammal to maintain this extrauterine life as a stopgap measure it is likely to be used in the interests of 'scientific advance'. Such is already possible in the veterinary world where a zebra has been delivered from a horse or donkey. Already a fetus has been cultured for seven weeks outside the uterus. The gap narrows.

It is not so much the fate of the individual human embryo that is disturbing as the sheer arrogance in the attempt to outdo the Almighty that must strike at the very hearts of Christian men and women. The acceptance of the principle that human life is expendable for whatever reason is the beginning of a slippery slope from which there may be no recovery.

Already, in Australia, there are over 250 frozen embryos in liquid nitrogen at minus 196 degrees C, a sort of emporium with presumably catalogued genetic details awaiting claimants or customers. Their ultimate disposal is being watched by many of us with interest, because they must be costing quite a lot to keep and maintain. They are obvious targets for research. Although the consumer demand for *in vitro* fertilisation is likely to increase, thanks to the latest methods of ovum retrieval by vaginal puncture and aspiration through a needle under ultrasonic guidance, research interests will clamour for the deliberate production of spare embryos (as has already happened in this city of Edinburgh).

Now I agree that it is difficult to get worked up about human life at the few cell stage when perfectly healthy babies (160,000 a year in England and Wales alone) are sacrificed annually often for the most trivial and non-medical reasons by the very people who weep their eyes out over the plight of the childless couple. There is money in a lot of this and the going-rate at the present seems to be around £2,000 an attempt at IVF and the usual 85 per cent failures can thereafter talk to their own bank managers. It is easy to think of the crocodile in *Alice in Wonderland*:

> How eagerly he seems to grin.
> How neatly spreads his claw
> And welcomes little fishes in with gently smiling jaws!

Let us turn our minds now, however, to the first of the big cracks in the leaky cistern already mentioned. I refer to the inclusion of a third party into the matrimonial relationship. It constitutes a very real threat to Christian life and the concept of the family and the sacrament of marriage. This third party intrusion so readily incorporated in artificial reproduction comes in one or more of four different forms which have already crept up on society to the extent of tacit approval.

First, and in some ways the most pernicious, is artificial insemination with donated semen (AID), the specimens being obtained from medical students by masturbation in return for a little cash. Here is a new cottage industry. What a lot has happened since the Archbishop of Canterbury condemned the practice so roundly in 1948. It has crept into acceptability, almost respectability, by stealth and a serious disregard for any really comprehensive control, including infection and the transmission, often unwitting, of serious genetic defect. The donor is rightly protected by anonymity and possibly by admixture with an infertile husband's sperm but apart from a few crude details about him – dark or fair, blue-eyed, tall or short and, of course, his ethnic group – there is little control or choice. I suppose apartheid operates here too. The child so conceived grows up under the shadow of a lie, compounded further on his birth certificate. These matters certainly troubled the Warnock Committee and their cruel remedy was to have the words 'by donation' against the 'father's' name on the birth certificate and that the child, by the age of 18, should have been told that the man he has grown up to love and admire as his father did not in fact beget him. Control is enjoined but it should be on a national scale computerised with every relevant genetic detail included as well as a very full medical examination to assess his fitness to father the next generation. Stock breeding, as in veterinary practice, will be the inevitable result. Even the recommended limitation in the number of donations could be by-passed by such a character hawking his services around different hospitals.

Needless to say I very vigorously opposed any such service being set up in my own department while in office. Enough said about a practice which only a humanist would accept, whatever his views about the aesthetic aspects.

Secondly comes donation of ova from a fertile woman to be fertilised *in vitro*. Here some sort of surgical assault is necessary to get at the ovum but plenty of opportunities arise in the course of other operations at the same time, *e.g.* sterilisation or hysterectomy. It is recommended that the 'consent' of the woman be first obtained but it would be even easier just to help oneself. Large numbers of ova can be harvested by first overstimulating the pituitary gland with hormones producing superovulation on the battery hen principle. The method will never be as numerically important as AID but the same ethical principles will apply.

The third type of intrusion brings up the question of surrogacy, now so much in the recent news. Adultery is as old as history itself but the earliest case of using it to achieve surrogate parenthood that comes to my mind is that of Abraham who was incited by Sarah to impregnate her slave woman Hagar in order to raise up seed for him. You will know the end of that story, and perhaps we are paying for it to this day!

As you know attempts are being made to set up an agency to employ women to go through pregnancy and childbirth, impregnated (perhaps) by the husband of an infertile couple anxious to acquire a baby at any price, currently about £24,000 of which the obliging mother only gets about £6,000, the agent who hired her womb pocketing the rest for one purpose or another. It is not against the law, since no law yet exists and already the practice is well established in the USA.[1] In last month's case the baby was made a ward of court but was nevertheless got out of the country outside the jurisdiction of the English courts. The organisation for this was brisk and highly efficient and the infertile couple appear to have got their 'child', the agent her fee and the surrogate mother the pittance which she required for doing up her house. There is very dangerous precedent here and until something can be decided about it rich, infertile American couples could repeat the procedure and thereby improve our dollar earnings by what could amount to the export of living human babies. The final national insult will come when the Soviet Union also enters the field to bolster up our failing currency by bidding in roubles!

The idea that a baby is a 'property', negotiable at that, is repugnant to most of the world which turned its back on slavery long ago before 'civilisation' lost its sense and sensibility and came to equate wanting with having. The Warnock Committee were indeed unhappy about commercial surrogacy and would like it made an offence, for doctors as well as agents. But the difficulties of enforcement by the law are formidable and driven underground the earnings would not even be available to the Inland Revenue any more than those of prostitution.

Lastly, there is human embryo transfer. In the veterinary world the first successful transfer of rabbit embryos was achieved as long ago as 1890 and the procedure had become commonplace by 1920 and made it possible to reduce freight costs to distant countries of very valuable farming stock whose progeny could be exported without hazarding the valuable stock animals. It soon extended to getting large numbers of genetically desirable lambs or calves born, following embryo transfer to common or garden and expendable surrogate mothers. If com-

---

1. The law was of course subsequently changed in the United Kingdom to outlaw commercial surrogacy.

bined with super-ovulation as already mentioned of the original mothers the profit yield could be enormous.

With the latest Swedish technique using the overfull urinary bladder to straighten out the human birth canal, which otherwise has a right-angled kink in it, this operation can be carried out as an outpatient. All that is necessary is a woman who believes herself likely to be pregnant from insemination, hopefully by the husband of the infertile couple four days earlier. Simple flushing out of her womb and collection of the early unimplanted embryo enables a transfer to the recipient uterus there and then, and if the aspiring mother-to-be was at the wrong stage of the menstrual cycle freeze storage could be adopted until the timing which is critical is suitable. There are snags, of course. Firstly the impregnated woman may be found not to have an embryo after all and she will then have been flushed out to no purpose, or the embryo may not come away so easily, leaving her with an unwelcome pregnancy with abortion on demand as her main option. There are too the risks of complications such as infection. Therefore money as recompense is bound to come into it, and this has already happened in the USA.

In that country an attempt to set up a lucrative business centre, complete with patent application (not yet granted) is already afoot anticipating 30,000 to 50,000 applicants at a suggested $10,000 per patient. This would promise a very brisk turn-over. So far the results are not very good, only 12 out of 29 reported attempts in one series gaining a proper foothold in pregnancy with considerably worse final results in terms of live births but the technique is still very new. One obvious attraction is that it might obviate the need for *in vitro* fertilisation since this would have already occurred in the donor uterus.

It is quite clear that in trying to meet the problem of childlessness for which IVF was originally designed in infertile marriages an enormous crop of ugly possibilities has been opened up. AID came upon us unprepared to control it and is, from the Christian point of view, totally unacceptable, whereas there is a legitimate case for IVF as a solution to overcoming infertility due to incurable tubal blockage in a wife.

Events are likely to overtake legislative action to try to contain the worst evils. It is suggested therefore as minimum measures we should press for the following:

Suspension of all research on living human embryos at all stages. This would effectively stop publication in scientific journals at home as well as abroad for fear of prosecution.

There should be no NHS funding for research institutions which anyway are largely staffed not by doctors, but by science workers who are not subject to the disciplinary control of the General Medical Council.

The charitable status of institutions attempting to get under the legal fence should be withdrawn.

All AID donors should be screened properly as to genetic antecedents and relevant transmissible diseases, *e.g.* AIDS. Details should be maintained on a national register, although preserving their anonymity.

Animal experimentation should be scrupulously monitored insofar as it might be misapplied to the human species.

Surely Christians, Catholic and Protestant, Muslims and Jews, could stand up and with one voice cry out 'Enough is enough'.

Yes, getting on for 3000 years ago, Jeremiah got it right. 'For my people have committed two evils: they have forsaken me, the fountain of living waters and hewn them out cisterns, broken cisterns that can hold no water.'

RESPONSES TO WARNOCK: A REVIEW

ISOBEL GRIGOR

My task in presenting a review of the various denominations' responses to Warnock is to consider how the churches have applied those insights within their role as witnesses and advocates of the Christian faith, and to consider what challenges remain.

I have studied the responses and, where possible, the submissions of the following bodies to the Report of the Warnock Committee: the Baptist Union of Scotland, the Catholic Bishops' Joint Committee on Bioethical Issues, the Church of England Board for Social Responsibility, the Church of Scotland Board of Social Responsibility, the Free Church of Scotland, the Free Church Federal Council, the Free Presbyterian Church of Scotland, the Methodist Church Division of Social Responsibility, (and also the Royal College of General Practitioners, and the Royal College of Nursing). Other denominations approached, for instance the Congregational Union and the United Free Church, were unable to supply copies of any responses. The focus of this paper will be mainly on the response of Scottish based denominations to the Warnock Report. The Report of the Catholic Bishops' Joint Committee straddles the border and the reference is made to the reports of the Church of England and Methodist Church as these will be recognised as significant contributions to the discussion of such issues within the Christian Church.[1]

One's first impression on studying the responses to the recommendations of the Warnock Committee from the above range of denominations is of the extent of agreement to be found between the churches in Scotland. While there may be differences in the expression of points or subsidiary matters, there is agreement on the central issues raised in the Report, relating to the sanctity of human life and the exclusivity of the marriage relationship. Indeed, if anything, the differences in presentation, reflecting different traditions, tend to draw attention to different

---

1. Readers are urged to obtain a copy of their own and other denominations' comments on the Warnock Report, for private study.

aspects of the Report, and to complement one another, adding to the quality of the combined response.

The central issue, on which there is common agreement among Scottish churches, concerns experimentation on human embryos. A misgiving shared by all the churches lies in the Report's side-stepping of moral questions leading to recommendations with which, in the words of the response of the Church of Scotland Board of Social Responsibility, 'It is impossible to sympathise ... without conceding issues of principle which the church believes to be of fundamental importance.' These issues are to do with the status of the human embryo and the marriage relationship as an institution ordained by God.

The basis of the moral arguments presented by the different denominations is summarised within the Church of Scotland response:

> 1. The Christian perspective starts from the position that human beings have been created by God and are loved by God. Made 'in the image of God and after his likeness', man is unique and has been endowed with faculties which enable him to enter into a personal relationship with his creator, and undertake responsibility for the creation on behalf of and alongside his creator. However, it is not just to the creative activity of God we must look, but to the Incarnation and his saving activity. God in Christ underlines not only the uniqueness of man, but the attitude of God, which is that his love does not depend on our achievements or abilities. The value of human life and the dignity of life derive from how God regards and treats us, and not from any status which legal or moral codes and conventions may confer at particular ages and stages of development. Thus, human beings may never treat each other as means to ends, but only as ends, and as ends backed by the ultimate sanction of God's being and love incarnate in Jesus Christ. No human being at any stage in his or her development may be treated in a way that violates his/her distinctively human nature and status, or subjects him/her to being a means to an end, even when that end is the greater health and happiness of other beings.
>
> 2. From the moment of conception the human embryo is genetically complete. It is an 'organised, unique, living unity with intrinsic capacity for development, human in character from its beginning' (Dr Teresa Iglesias). The moral status of the embryo and its moral claim on us do not diminish the further back we go in the stages of its development. From the moment of fertilisation it has the right to be protected and treated as a human being. There is 'a serious ambiguity about an argu-

ment from the premise that the embryo is 'potentially human', for the potentiality concerned is not that of becoming something else but of becoming what it essentially is. (Professor T.F. Torrance).

With the exception of the Church of England and Methodist Church all the denominations listed above have put forward arguments based on the sanctity of human life to oppose experimentation on human embryos which is not intended for the good of the embryos involved.

A major objection to experimentation on human embryos, stemming from a belief in their essential humanity, is the view put forward that it is not acceptable to use any human being simply as a means to an end. The 1975 Declaration of Helsinki (WHO) is widely quoted: 'In research on man the interests of science and society should never take precedence over considerations related to the well-being of the subject.' Although the Warnock Report rejects the charge that it is based on a utilitarian ethic, its defence cuts little ice with the churches. The argument is developed most effectively by the Catholic Bishops' Committee, which sees in the priority given to the interests of infertile adults the use of children precisely as a means to an end. The result is, they say, a distortion of the human perspective.

The Inquiry's terms of reference were 'to consider recent and potential developments in medicine and science related to human fertilisation and embryology', and 'to consider what policies and safeguards should be applied . . . .' The Chairman's letter to the Government, which introduces the Report, foreshadows a subtle but quite fundamental shift of perspective. In that letter, 'fertilisation' and 'embryology' disappear from view, to be replaced by 'the field of human assisted reproduction'. In this shift of perspective, from the embryo to the infertile, the interests of embryo and child, *i.e.* of the new human being who is either being envisaged and planned for or who actually exists, are systematically subordinated to the interests of the adults who (very understandably) want a child. And those interests and rights of the newly generated are subordinated to the optimisation of a technique for fulfilling that adult want. The moral rights of the embryo, and the moral rights and wrongs of IVF and artificial insemination, are issues submerged or at least distorted by the Inquiry's primary concern with techniques for meeting an adult need.

The churches' opposition to embryo research also relates to the deliberate wastage of human embryos and to a concern that IVF techniques may provide the opportunity for embryo selection and the discarding of unwanted or unacceptable embryos. A dilemma arising from current practice is demonstrated in the response of the Church of Scotland Board of Social Responsibility in commenting on superovulation resulting in the production of spare embryos. These, it is suggested, should be disposed of rather than put to alternative uses. The Free Presbyterian Church of Scotland and the Catholic Bishops have expressed their opposition to the promotion of IVF on the grounds that it is basically an experimental technique involving a significant risk of failure during implantation and the predictable wastage of embryos.

When to the churches' opposition to experimentation is added the opposition of such groups as the Royal College of Nursing (totally against experimentation), and the Royal College of General Practitioners (opposed to experimentation in their submission, but more divided in their response), and the fact that three members of the Warnock Committee rejected experimentation in principle and another four rejected the production of embryos specifically for the purpose of research – it is clear that concern and opposition to experimentation on human embryos has to be taken seriously in any legislation following on the Warnock Report. The reaction of these various groups brings into question issues which strike at the heart of the Warnock Report itself.

The extent of agreement between the churches regarding their approach to the embryo is found also in their reaction to the Report's recommendations regarding the development of infertility treatment. Views differ as to whether AID is actually adulterous but there is unanimous rejection of third party donation on ethical grounds as an intrusion into the marriage relationship and an acute concern for the practical consequences of such techniques. The Warnock Committee is supported by the churches in its concern over surrogacy and its recommendation that organised surrogacy be made illegal, although in some responses social or psychological reasons are stressed while in others concern surrounds the fact that surrogacy strikes at the essence and dignity of the woman as created by God.

The pragmatism of the Report – in seeking to provide the means by which now established practices may be continued – is also attacked by the churches. The point is made by the Baptist Union and the Free Church of Scotland, for instance, that it is concerned both in terms of research and development in fertility treatment, not with the moral choices involved. In addition, it is pointed out, the Report lacks any discussion of relative priority in developments in health care. Isolation of its subjects from their wider context and the presentation of infertility as a basic human need mean that questions concerning the allocation of health services resources, and the development of alternative means of responding to infertility not involving donation, or even serious consideration of the underlying causes of infertility, are neglected.

As the Free Church of Scotland has argued:

> There is no doubt that the emotional, psychological and marital problems which can result from infertility, are very real and the development of techniques to overcome the problem is to be welcomed. If, however, a priority list of major world-wide medical problems were to be made, infertility would come relatively low down on such a list. In addition, in vitro fertilisation will only provide a solution in those cases of infertility due to tubal blockage. In these days of limited and declining financial resources, programmes for in vitro fertilisation must carry relatively low priority. We feel that there is a danger that the clinical importance of the problem has been exaggerated by medical scientists to allow them greater access to a potentially most exciting research tool.

The responses to the Warnock Report from the Anglican and Methodist Churches in England differ significantly from those of the Scottish churches. Within the Church of England discussion of issues arising from the Report has led to a long and contentious debate. The majority view in a report from the Board for Social Responsibility that experimentation on human embryos be permitted up to 14 days – but that embryos should not be produced for experimentation, in line with Note of Dissent C – was rejected by Synod in February 1985. Subsequent discussion in dioceses is focussing now on a further Social Responsibility report called *Personal Origins*. Given the strength of the debate within the Church of England, it would appear that opinion on this matter is fairly equally divided with groups both convinced for and against experimentation and third party donation, but with a number in-between who may use the opportunity provided by the *Personal Origins* report to come to an understanding of the issues.

The Methodists have aligned themselves with the Anglicans, as reported in the *Methodist Recorder* of 10 January 1985:

> Each welcomed the insistence of Warnock that the human embryo must have some protection in law, but each, by majority vote, agreed with the recommendation that strictly controlled experimentation should be permitted within the first 14 days of conception. The Methodist response quoted the Statement on Abortion approved by the conference in 1976. 'All human life ... should be reverenced. The foetus is undoubtedly part of the continuum of human existence, but the Christian will wish to study further the extent to which the foetus is a person.'

Underlying the recommendation that experimentation be permitted up to 14 days after conception, as proposed by Warnock, is a fundamentally different outlook on the embryo from that taken by the churches in Scotland. Whereas the Scottish churches have taken the view that the embryo be respected as a human person from the moment of conception, the Anglicans and Methodists have argued on the basis of a gradualist perspective that while the human embryo is very special, recognition of its humanness (and therefore the way in which it may be treated), is to be related to stages in its development as revealed in embryology.

> ... until the embryo has reached the first 14 days of its existence, it is not yet entitled to the same respect and protection as an embryo implanted in the human womb and in which individuation has begun.

The most obvious difficulty in taking up this position is the arbitrariness that it involves. At what stage in its development, and according to what criteria, are we to decide that the developing embryo has become a person? If not from its earliest stages, does not this decision tend to reflect the purposes and requirements of a particular treatment programme? Fetuses at similar stages of development may, for instance, find themselves as the focus of urgent peri-natal care to ensure viability, or the subject of termination. Professor John Marshall, a member of the Warnock Committee, speaking at an earlier Rutherford House Conference, talked of the arbitrariness of the 14 day limit on experimentation. This was, he said, a pragmatic compromise worked out between members who opposed experimentation on ethical grounds and others who wished to unlock the knowledge which they believed experimentation would provide.

Humanity is not something to be conferred on the developing fetus depending on the availability of resources or relative to treatment or research priorities, or parental wishes. It is there in the fetus, though we may choose not to recognise it. Human personhood is conferred by God in the act of creating a new human life. His followers are called to act responsibly towards his creation recognising its status in his eyes.[1] Development is the mark of human growth, extending into mature adulthood. How, then, are we to justify attributing greater significance to some individuals rather than others according to the stage of their development? Similar questions are obviously arising towards the end of life, when decisions have to be made regarding treatment. This is an urgent question which our society must probe in recognition of the moral issues underlying developments in contemporary research and medicine.

It is to be hoped that in reflecting on responses received from the churches to the Warnock Report, those responsible for legislation will appreciate the need to look critically at the attitude towards fetal life on which it is based. It would be a mistake to overlook the strength of opposition within the Scottish churches to the practice of experimentation. This would be to underestimate also the seriousness of discussion continuing within the churches in England regarding the embryo's status. Following the Anglican Church's decision on this matter, the *Methodist Recorder* reflected on current debate:

> Our own view is that the Church of Scotland is right to maintain that 'the status of the embryo' is the heart of the problem. On this we incline to the opinion that genetic research has provided a great deal of evidence for the further study envisaged by the Conference of 1976, and that the balance of the evidence tends to the judgement that the embryo is human. Our Scottish friends are better scientists and better theologians.

---

1. For discussion of this point, see for instance T.F. Torrance, *Test Tube Babies,* Edinburgh, 1984.

The widely held concern within the Christian community for developments in the area of embryo experimentation demonstrates the inadequacy of the Warnock Report in its reluctance 'to appear to dictate on matters of morals to the public at large' (page 1, paragraph 2). The Report was concerned with issues which are inescapably of moral significance, and in seeking to pursue some perception of 'the common good', and in making concessions to a pluralistic society, the Committee has failed to address fundamental questions. The combined responses of the churches provide an important contribution to this discussion and it is to be hoped that their relevance will be appreciated in any consideration of the findings of this Committee.

Challenges Facing the Church

1. Every effort must be made to ensure that the views of Christians are represented clearly in future Parliamentary discussion of legislation on human fertilisation and embryology.

2. The opportunity should be taken within denominations to develop serious discussion amongst their members of the moral and ethical issues raised by the Warnock Report. The preparation of study and discussion material for congregational groups and individual study would be of great assistance. As a first step members might be encouraged to obtain copies of their denomination's comments on the Warnock Report and use these as the basis for discussion. Consideration of such issues should form a normal part of Christian education within the life of the congregation. Ideally, young people should be given opportunities to consider moral and ethical questions as they grow up within the Christian faith, for they should not be expected to think about the morality of such emotional and traumatic issues for the first time when they are personally affected by the prospect of a handicapped child, congenital abnormality, or the problems of infertility.

3. In some ways the easier task for the Christian church is to produce reports and comments on specific issues. The more difficult task for Christian people is to live in the world serving their Lord faithfully, bringing his healing touch to those who are in need, and even being true in their own lives to what they believe. Hereditary disease, handicap, and infertility are amongst the most perplexing and emotive of human problems, drawing

on individuals' and couples' deepest resources either in facing these for themselves or in helping others directly affected. In recognition of this, the Royal College of General Practitioners in its response to the Warnock Report has drawn attention to the need for GPs to be trained to provide the support and counselling which couples require. The way in which these are met by Christian people will speak loudly of their faith and of God. Through their dealings with other people an image can be conveyed of God as either a cruel and capricious God who grants children to some but not to others, like favours, and who deals out handicap and illness almost like a punishment - or as a loving God who wants only good for his people.

It is important that Christian people as individuals and as members of congregations should meet together to consider the deeply personal issues covered in reports like this and talk about how they would face them in their own lives and how they would hope to help others.[3] Opportunities could be provided for childless couples or for parents with handicapped children to meet together to discuss how they face these situations in the light of their Christian faith. Thought should be given within the life of the whole congregation to the particular contribution to the Christian family which is made by handicapped people, by childless couples, the single, *etc*. - and also to their needs. Doctors and other members of the congregation whose work involves such moral questions could be invited to meet together and with the congregation as a whole to talk about questions which affect them all as Christian people.

---

3. A most helpful resource for congregational discussion or individual study is *Choices in Childlessness*, the report of a Working Party set up in July 1979 under the auspices of the Free Church Federal Council and the British Council of Churches - obtainable from the Free Church Federal Council, 27 Tavistock Square, London, WC1H 9HH, for 80p.

AFTER THE EMBRYO THE FETUS?

SIR JOHN PEEL

When I began my medical career as a student over sixty years ago I was introduced to the subject of Embryology by the then Professor of Anatomy at Oxford. Embryology was his prime interest. In his lectures he took us through, with methodical precision, all the stages of development from the fertilised ovum, in the fallopian tube, to its ultimate expulsion from the uterus as a full-term child.

If there was one fact he used to impress on all his students time and time again, it was that a new life began at conception – that all the developmental changes that took place thereafter were part of a continuum that went on for the whole duration of the pregnancy. There are of course many landmarks, each denoting progression, which can be picked out during the course of intra-uterine life, which are significant – both subjectively and objectively; but their recognition does not alter the fundamental fact that it is at the moment of conception, when the sperm penetrates the ovum, that a new vital spark is given to the single-celled ovum which endows it with the potential to create a new human being. Some distinguished scientists have argued that after fertilisation, as the ovum begins to divide and multiply its cellular formation, it remains a simple mass of cells, a morula, which cannot be regarded as even a potential human being, because half of those cells are given to form merely the placenta and membranes, and it is only with the appearance of the primitive streak that the new embryo becomes recognisable. This I think is only a half truth because the other half of the cells really are destined to form the new fetus. After all, in these terms what are any of us, as adults, but a mass of millions of cells. The statement therefore that life begins at conception and not only after fourteen days or thereafter, is not simply an anti-abortionist moral stance, but is scientifically indisputable. Perhaps I could quote from a more modern embryologist, Dr David Woollam, who at the launching of the Helsinki Medical Group in London said:

The Warnock Committee appears to have reached the view on the allowability of experiment on the human embryo by starting with the fertilised ovum and then working forwards to a time when they felt that experimentation was no longer acceptable. I prefer to look backwards in time from the birth of a normal healthy child. As I travel back in the life history of the fetus and embryo to the point of formation of the zygote I find, as an embryologist, that there is no moment in time at which I can say Yes, this must be the stage when it changed from a non-human being to a human being.

I find that the choice of fourteen days as a cut-off point before which anything by way of disposal or experimentation goes, whereas after that date nothing is to be allowed, is a choice that has no real scientific, moral or practical basis. We have lived through an era of thirty to forty years in which there has been a graduation, a progression by stealth, in most aspects of individual and social behaviour. What was unacceptable thirty years ago is taken as common-place today. Whether progression is always progress is a matter of opinion - in many areas I would regard it as deterioration. The erosion of discipline, not so much external discipline, but self-discipline, of responsibility for personal actions and personal life-style, is clear for all to see. I think it is naive in the extreme to imagine that fourteen days relating to experiments on human embryos will be adhered to for very long, whether carried out legally or illegally. Already a number of scientists working in this field have expressed the view that this date-line should be extended to twenty-eight days and beyond. And if you believe in experimenting on human embryos, you have logic on your side in taking this view. No-one can tell the end result of any research programme, and I have little doubt that when the time comes that the *in vitro* embryo can be kept alive and growing for fourteen days and beyond the experimenters will want to go on. And once you breach a fundamental principle of ethics, why shouldn't they? We have been through the era of sexual revolution, with abortion, originally for serious medical and social reasons, and now free for all, with contraception for married women with large families and now for pre-teenagers. We are now beginning the era of the reproductive revolution, with veterinary principles entering into the field of human reproduction. Is this what society wants?

AFTER THE EMBRYO THE FETUS?

In 1970, when considerable concern was finding expression in the public about the disposal of the thousands of fetuses that became suddenly available as a result of the Abortion Act 1967, I was asked by the then Minister of Health to chair a working group to consider the ethical, medical, social and legal implications of using the fetus and fetal material for research. Much has, of course, happened since then. IVF. was, if I may so use the expression in this context, very much in an embryonic stage of development. Some of our conclusions might not be applicable today, but much of our report dealt with matters that are as relevant today as they were then. At the outset we found difficulty in regard to some of the definitions in general usage - embryo, fetus, pre-viable and viable fetuses. After reviewing all the evidence we came to the conclusion that the 'fetus' was the human embryo from conception to delivery - and nobody at that time questioned the validity of that definition. I think it is important. It concentrates the mind and clarifies the debate to appreciate that the embryo is simply the fetus in the earliest stages of its development, and not a separate entity to be disposed of at will. I make no apology therefore in discussing briefly ethics and fetuses, because they include embryos.

There are no ethical problems involved in making use of fetal material or the dead fetus expelled from the uterus by spontaneous or therapeutic abortion. There is a question about which opinions differ - whether there should or should not be any statutory obligation to seek the consent of the woman herself if it is intended to make use of the material for research or therapeutic purposes - or indeed whether a woman who has consented to have the fetus she is carrying killed by abortion has any right to exercise any control over what is done with the fetus afterwards.[1]

For a great many years research has been conducted in the areas of virology, cancer research, immunology and in relation to congenital deformities, with very significant and beneficial results. At the other end of the scale it would be unethical and unacceptable to carry out research on the viable fetus after deliv-

---

1. Refer to our report: *Report of the Advisory Group on the Use of Fetuses and Fetal Material for Research*, DHSS, 1972

ery, except in so far as any research consisted of the results of the application of any new technique or the exhibition of a new therapy designed to treat a condition for which the neonate was suffering, with a view to assisting its recovery or prolonging its life. The real ethical problems arise in regard to what is spoken of as a pre-viable fetus. Enshrined in the Infant Life Preservation Act 1929 is the definition of a viable fetus as one that is 'capable of being born alive'. That Act gives blanket protection to the fetus from deliberate injury from conception to delivery, save under the provisions of the Abortion Act 1967; and further that protection is not abrogated by the fact that it may be the intention at the time of the infliction of the injury that the fetus should be prevented by subsequent abortion from attaining life. So in law you can kill the fetus but you must not inflict any injury upon it. Hence there *is* a need for clarification of the law and some more precise definition of viability and what is meant by 'capable of being born alive', which is a very imprecise phrase.

During the past two decades such advances in neonatal paediatrics have been made that more and more fetuses born prematurely can now be kept alive by the application of new techniques, and the degree of prematurity is becoming earlier and earlier, but without the application of such medical care the fetus is no more 'capable of being born alive' than it was previously. A fetus expelled at, say, sixteen to eighteen weeks will, unless it has already died, have a detectable heart-beat and make respiratory gasps. There is no possibility of it surviving even with all that scientific medicine has to offer at present, but its basic life process can be kept going for a brief period, perhaps an hour or more. It is here that the scientist argues that if such a fetus is certain to die in such a short time, why not keep it going as long as possible so that we can do useful experiments. Alternatively, prior to the abortion why not give to the mother drugs, chemical substances, *etc.* which will not damage the mother but may pass through the placenta to affect the fetus. In that way it might help to know just how and why different fetal organs become affected. The Abortion Act has unhappily lowered the status of the fetus in the eyes of both doctors and the public and to many it seems totally illogical that society allows in this country alone upwards of 150,000 fetuses to be killed every year, and raises serious and fierce debate about the fate of an embryonic fetus during the first fourteen days of its life. It is indeed illogical. But it is an issue that raises such fundamental questions on all aspects of human experimentation.

I make no apology for having spoken at some length about the problems of experimentation on the fetus conceived *in vivo* both before and after it leaves the mother's uterus, because these problems are closely related to those of experimentation on the human fetus (embryo) conceived *in vitro*. To raise the spectre of ectogenesis runs the risk of being accused of scare-mongering in the realms of science fiction. But as research progresses into the creation of the artificial womb, what purpose can there be in it if not to take the first steps towards the ultimate of ectogenesis? Scientific, technological and clinical developments are proceeding at such a rapid rate that clearly once fertilisation *in vitro* has been accomplished, efforts will be made to prolong the life span of the embryo - while at the other end of the scale fetuses delivered prematurely at earlier and earlier stages of development will survive. Will a time come when the two extremes may meet? There is developing a whole new field of fetal medicine which is not only exciting scientifically but is of great practical clinical value. The new techniques of monitoring the fetus throughout its period of intra-uterine life are no longer confined to diagnosis, but are being extended to beneficial therapy. Intra-uterine blood transfusion was the first in this field, but now a variety of operative as well as diagnostic procedures are possible. My only anxiety is that the opportunities for experimentation must occur and it would be tragic if such a beneficial development should become at risk of being abused. And make no mistake it will be abused if the standards of human experimentation are relaxed.

Since the Warnock Report was published so much has been written and spoken about it, both for and against, that it becomes difficult to find issues that have not been debated very fully already. However there are three or four aspects that I should like to speak about now. Let us take one problem of infertility. It is frequently stated that it is only by means of *in vitro* fertilisation and research on embryos that infertility can be cured. Infertility has always been with us and most couples unfortunate enough to find themselves in this situation have learned to live with it. In my experience the absence of children has seldom led to the break-up of a marriage (a relationship, to use the current phraseology) if that has been firmly based in marital love and devotion. And seldom has a rocky marriage been secured by pregnancy. But with the advent of *in vitro* fertilisation, it has become, in a sense, glamorised. Many women having won the right to discard the fetus at will have then had expectations to have their infertility cured at will. The whole subject has, so to speak, hit the headlines. IVF was of course first popularised as the best means of relieving infertility in a very special and restricted group of women - those whose fallopian tubes had become obstructed due to previous infection. It was indeed a tremendous technological medical achievement and full recognition of this fact is freely acknowledged by us all. Unhappily due to the current climate of sexual mores there has been a considerable increase in sexually transmitted diseases and so more women, otherwise fertile, have become infertile by reason of tubal blockage compounded by early sterilisation.

However, IVF remains a technique at present complicated and not highly efficient, albeit the best even if not the only way of alleviating the infertility in these cases. A recent report from Australia records a series of 244 pregnancies established after *in vitro* fertilisation - in which 27 per cent ended in spontaneous abortion, 22 per cent in multiple births, 5 per cent in tubal pregnancies and a three times higher incidence of pre-term births than in the general population. Both premature births and multiple births greatly increase the physical and mental risks in those babies that survive as they progress into childhood and adolescence. It is often alleged that those of us who are expressing grave concern at the new technology of artificial reproduction are callous about the plight of infertile couples anxious to have a child, and further it is argued that only by IVF can a cure for infertility be found. Both allegations are totally untrue, and my concern is not with the application of *in vitro* fertilisation to suitably selected infertile couples, but to its extension and possible abuse outside this narrow field of application. We should not confine our attention too strictly to the question of embryo research, but see it in the context of this whole new field of artificial reproduction - AID, egg donation, surrogacy, as well as *in vitro* fertilisation.

These techniques can be and are being extended outside marriage - even to single women with no male partner, who are anxious to have a child, but who wish to avoid involvement with any member of the opposite sex, moral, emotional or legal. Are the wishes of the individual woman always to be paramount? It is not for doctors to provide answers to such a question, but I believe society should give far more serious consideration to the direction in which we are moving and consider whether it is not laying the foundations of problems to come. Those problems concern something so far largely ignored and scant concern has been expressed about the product of these procedures - namely the child. How will many children as they grow into adolescence, conceived in these artificial circumstances, regard the dignity of their origins? In the days when there were many babies available for adoption, prior to the Abortion Act, it was commonly accepted that at the age of 18 it was right for every adopted child to know the details of its birth. The Houghton Committee in 1972, set up to consider adoption, stated that the interests of the child should always take precedence over the requirements of the adopting couple. How is this principle to be applied, for example, in the case of children artificially conceived outside the normal family situation? And because when IVF is employed, it is necessary to implant more than a single embryo, the risks of multiple pregnancy are greatly increased. I find the production of six babies, instead of one, as occurred in one case, positively obscene. Instead of being regarded as a medical failure, it was glamorised as a triumph with pictures in the newspapers of a whole army of doctors, nurses and paramedical staff who had been employed in the whole procedure. What is to be the future of those six babies? One cannot help wondering - not to mention the reactions of the parents as time passes.

Reverting to the problem of infertility, it is important to remember that the causes of infertility are many and varied and that the whole range of these new techniques of artificial reproduction is aimed at alleviating the condition and is not directed in any way to elucidating the causes. I think therefore that there is a great danger that if they are adopted too widely and too easily, they may inhibit alternative research and the development of treatments likely to cure rather than alleviate. There is a whole range of conditions responsible for infertility, which it would be inappropriate to discuss within this context, but great strides have been made in many conditions and it would be wrong to imagine that artificial means are the only ones likely to benefit the infertile couple. The second claim that is often repeated is that it is only by experimentation on the embryo that the results of IVF can be improved and abnormalities in the fetus prevented.

It is, of course, the word 'experimentation' on the human embryo (fetus) that creates so much emotion and moral indignation; and quite rightly, because experimentation on the human is by common consent, only to be undertaken if designed to help the subject, but not simply to increase knowledge or benefit science and society. It is important to recognise that observation is an integral part of research, and it would not be right to criticise the observation of the embryo created *in vitro*, up to the time when it is judged optimum for implantation into the uterus. That is not experimentation, and it seems to me perfectly ethical to observe the embryo fertilised *in vitro* and to make every effort to improve the medium in which the embryo develops prior to insertion into the uterus. But the biggest problem is not so much the fertilisation of the ovum *in vitro*, but the embedding in the uterus. There is only a 15 per cent success and that is why it is necessary to implant several embryos, and why the causes of failure are maternal rather than fetal - and experimentation on the embryo seems unlikely to make the procedure more successful. But much more is contemplated by the scientific researchers. No-one can foretell the ultimate outcome of any research programme, and that is why it is impossible to prove or disprove the validity of any claim that may be made about the potential benefits likely to come from any particular piece of research. In the matter of embryo research the experts disagree. Even if those experts who argue that it is research on the gametes prior to fertilisation that is more necessary than research on the embryo, appear to be in a minority, it is not to say they are wrong, and I for one agree with them on general principles and on my clinical experience. We all want the elimination of genetic diseases, but not I hope at any price. Maternal and environmental factors are more important causes of handicap and disability in children than are genetic diseases, but that does not mean that every effort should not be made to eliminate hereditary factors. It is a question of the most likely avenue for research and I do not believe that experimentation on the embryo is the most profitable line to be pursued.

If embryo research is to be permitted, albeit only for fourteen days, will not very large numbers be required? Spare embryos from infertile couples will never satisfy the needs and so we face the practice, in my view entirely unethical, of inducing multiple ovulation in the ovaries of volunteer women due to have some gynaecological operation - collecting them by laparoscopy or other techniques and fertilising them with sperm from any source available. I find this procedure repugnant and so I think will the vast majority of women.

It is claimed that amongst other benefits likely to emerge from research on human embryos is the reduction in the incidence of early embryonic death and spontaneous abortion. The Medical Research Council in its response to the Warnock Report was reported as saying that one million conceptions are lost every year before pregnancy is established and 100,000 spontaneous abortions occur due to chromosomal abnormality. Both these figures, especially the first, seem to have been plucked out of the air. Surely there must be millions of sperms, near exhaustion towards the end of their journey to the female genital tract after seven or eight days, meeting up with the ova beginning to disintegrate, and small wonder if conception occurs it is unlikely to progress. How could such an event be prevented, except by confining sexual intercourse to the optimum period of 12 to 24 hours in the life of the ovum, to the whole human race? And even if it could, there would be either an unthinkable explosion in the population or a vast increase in the demand for abortion. In my experience I would argue that maternal and environmental factors are more important causes of spontaneous abortion than chromosomal abnormalities, and if they are the cause, is it not better that the conception be aborted spontaneously? The potential benefits from embryo research are, I think, exaggerated, but not being a scientist but a simple clinician I cannot prove it - nor can anyone else.

One final point - if embryo research is so vital and so necessary, why is it necessary to create such an elaborate means for monitoring and controlling it? Obviously to try to reduce the risk of abuse. And if opinion is so divided, what sort of licensing body can ever be created that would be truly impartial? And how could it possibly carry out its responsibilities in every detail? The controlling mechanism established after the 1967 Abortion Act failed almost completely to function in the way originally intended, and I fear that the same fate would befall any licensing body set up to try to control this whole new field of reproductive techniques.

I am aware that the objective of this conference is to produce a Christian view of all the issues covered by the Warnock Report. For that reason I have deliberately strayed away from the narrow field of ethics and embryos. I am no theologian but do profess Christian convictions relating to this whole field of artificial reproduction. I find the oft repeated statement that it is only those of the Catholic faith who are opposed to the recommendations of the Warnock Report, not only grossly inaccurate but offensive to those of us who, though not of the Catholic faith, hold strong convictions and who are profoundly worried by the deterioration of moral standards in so many aspects of contemporary life. Do we really believe that the introduction of some of the principles and practices applicable to the veterinary world, if introduced widely in the area of human reproduction, will enhance the dignity and status of the human race? Let us have by all means compassion for the infertile couple, but let us not become obsessed with physical perfection as the only goal to be aimed at. Human sperm, ova, embryos, are frozen, banked and stored in so many places - if this is allowed to continue how will the dignity of human reproduction be maintained? How will Christian marriage survive and the family remain a pivotal entity in our society? How will some of the children, who having been deliberately deceived about the mode of their origin, react when they learn the truth? Is this Pandora's box when opened not liable to lead to such a confusion of moral, social and legal problems that will not be capable of resolution? If the tide is to be turned it will be on a moral and not a scientific stance.

I would like to conclude by quoting a letter which I and a number of other gynaecologists wrote to *The Times*, which epitomises my views better than I can do in any other way.

AFTER THE EMBRYO THE FETUS?

Sir,

As Fellows of the Royal College of Obstetricians and Gynaecologists, we consider that those recommendations of the Warnock Committee relating to embryo research reduce the status of the human embryo to that of an experimental animal, contravene the code of medical ethics and must be rejected.

The rejection of experimentation on human embryos is implicit in the code of professional ethics, relating to all human experimentation, which has from time immemorial been endorsed by the medical profession and repeatedly confirmed by the World Medical Association and other professional bodies. The central principle of this code is that concern for the interests of the subject, namely the patient, must always prevail over the interests of science or society. The human embryo conceived by *in vitro* fertilisation is the subject of the doctor's concern, and as with an adult patient, may not be put at risk for any reason other than to enhance his or her own well-being.

The effective investigation of pathological conditions developing during pre-natal life should not require the killing of human embryos. Indeed primary prevention of many such conditions, as opposed to their secondary prevention by killing those who suffer them, is more likely to be achieved by applying new techniques of research to human gametes and not to human embryos.

CHILDLESS COUPLES AND ROOTLESS CHILDREN

RICHARD HIGGINSON

Most of the practices on which the Warnock Report comments pre-dated its work by some years. Artificial Insemination by Donor has been practised in this country since the Second World War and has been quite widely, if unevenly, available since 1960. The birth of the first 'test-tube' baby, Louise Brown, in 1978 followed nearly a decade of research into *in vitro* fertilisation. Public attention on the field of artificial insemination and embryology seems to have increased considerably after that dramatic event. In fact the IVF pioneers Robert Edwards and Patrick Steptoe had been requesting legislative guidelines in an unclear situation for many years; but it was not until July 1982 that a Committee of Inquiry was set up

> To consider recent and potential developments in medicine and science related to human fertilisation and embryology; to consider what policies and safeguards should be applied, including consideration of the social, ethical and legal implications of these developments; and to make recommendations.[1]

The Committee worked quickly, and published its Report in June 1984. Chapters 3 and 8 of the Report are headed 'Techniques for the Alleviation of Infertility'. It is a curious use of the word *alleviation.* One would have thought that a more accurate description of these techniques is the overcoming of childlessness or the circumvention of infertility. This is not just a semantic point, because it draws attention to a curious omission in the Report. The Report cites the familiar estimate that about one couple in ten are thought to suffer from infertility. It outlines the scope of the problem, while lamenting the lack of accurate statistics on the subject. But there is no exploration of the various reasons why some couples are unable to conceive children, other than mention of the purely physical factors which can lead in the direction of one artificial technique rather than

1. *Report of the Committee of Inquiry into Human Fertilisation and Embryology* (henceforth Warnock Report), para. 1.2.

another. Yet it would surely have been relevant to point out that psychological factors can affect the performance of the act of sexual intercourse, the emission of semen and therefore the chances of conception; that damage to a woman's fallopian tubes is often caused through the effects of a previous abortion, use of the coil as a contraceptive device, or sexually transmitted diseases; that sometimes there is no discernible reason why a couple cannot conceive (fertilisation being something of a random affair, certain couples are persistently unlucky). The intention of drawing attention to these factors would not be to heap scorn, blame or pity on the individuals concerned. Rather, attempting to identify the causes of infertility in particular cases should be the prelude to finding an appropriate therapy; and for some couples resort to sexual therapy, repair of the fallopian tubes or simply a willingness to go on trying would appear to be the appropriate step before artificial techniques for overcoming childlessness are seriously considered. Doubtless most couples do go through such preliminary stages first. What is strange is that the Report rushes on to the artificial techniques so quickly.

The fact remains that a substantial minority of couples, many of whom are in no sense to blame for their infertility problem, and even after resort to therapy of an appropriate kind, still find themselves saddled with the sad reality of childlessness. (There are of course some couples who choose not to have children, but one assumes them to be a minority within the category of childless couples.) There is no doubting that involuntary childlessness causes suffering. Part of the pressure to have children is a social pressure: it is something that most couples do, the joys and satisfactions which it brings usually seem to outweigh the strains and sorrows, and couples who do not have children clearly fall outside the social norm. The excitement that news of an expected birth brings to the extended family, especially grandparents, is paralleled by the disappointment caused by a failure to conceive. But a greater part of the pressure to conceive probably comes from within: individually and as a couple, the desires to perpetuate one's line and to consummate one's sexual relationship through the creation of a child whom one can nurture and cherish, are extremely strong human instincts.

Hairs have been split over whether the desire to bear children constitutes a need or a want. For most couples it is a want which, if unsatisfied, creates a deep emotional need. It is not of course crucial to life; nor should it be crucial to the survival of a loving marital relationship; but it leaves a huge hole amidst the realisations of the usual expectations of that relationship. Childlessness creates much misery, and if new techniques appear to hold out the hope of overcoming it, we are duty-bound to give them at the very least sympathetic consideration.

In the Bible, childlessness is viewed as a great human sorrow, and sometimes as a sign of divine disfavour.[2] But just as God takes away, so also he delights to give and to restore. The joy which Hannah experienced at the the birth of Samuel will find echoes in many couples who have thought they were infertile and then been pleasantly surprised to find otherwise! God's concern for the childless widow is shown in his provision of levirate marriage to ensure a progeny.[3]   Even resort by Abraham and Jacob to *natural* insemination of their barren wives' slave-girls is not recorded as meeting with God's disapproval. A Christian doctor who is sympathetic to Warnock's recommendations has suggested to me that 'Rachel and Sarah would be leaning over the battlements cheering Lady Warnock on at the moment'!

Because of the suffering which childlessness brings, and because of the obvious immediate joy which circumvention of infertility through the use of new artificial techniques has undeniably brought, the case for pressing ahead with these techniques and making them available as widely as possible is seen by some as unanswerable. To raise questions about the moral propriety and psychological advisability of resorting to such techniques is to run the risk of being accused of legalistic nit-picking and lack of compassion for the childless couple. It is especially difficult if one is oneself able to conceive children through natural means and appears to be saying 'No' to a pleasure that one has oneself been privileged to enjoy. Yet the case for pressing ahead should not be assumed to be proven incontestably too quickly. It is not just moral prudes or kill-joys who harbour

2. See *e.g.* Gen. 20:17-18, 2 Sam. 6:23.
3. See Deut. 25:5-6.

doubts about these techniques; indeed, the scruples of some childless couples are such that they are not prepared to resort to them. In the words of the Warnock Report, the reason why the Committee was set up was because

> Society's views on the new techniques were divided between pride in the technological achievement, pleasure at the new-found means to relieve, at least for some, the unhappiness of infertility, and unease at the apparently uncontrolled advance of science, bringing with it new possibilities for manipulating the early stages of human development.[4]

In short, there was anxiety about the implications of the new developments in assisted reproduction.

Yet although the Warnock Report refers to this anxiety at the outset, it is questionable whether that concern is adequately expressed or responded to in the main body of the Report. Much of that anxiety concerns the fate of those created by the artificial techniques: firstly embryos, and secondly children who are destined to become adults. It concerns the implications of this highly unusual start to human life for one's treatment and well-being thereafter. And it is an entirely pertinent criticism of the Warnock Committee that in their desire to meet the needs of adults caught in the distress of infertility they were insufficiently attentive to the likely effects that creation through artificial means has on the child itself. Of course conjecture about these effects is bound to be speculative, partly because many of the techniques are still in their infancy, and partly because one which has been around much longer (AID) has been shrouded in secrecy. Yet research has been done on AID families, and while it has unearthed many stories of apparently happy families with no regrets, it has also brought to light some sad tales which should act as warning lights to couples contemplating this or similar practices.[5]

In the paragraphs which follow I suggest certain ways in which children conceived through artificial techniques may be at risk. I stress the words 'may' and 'at risk'; the undesirable effects envisaged will certainly not ensue in every case. Also,

---

4. *Warnock Report*, 1.1.
5. See R. Snowden and G. D. Mitchell, *The Artificial Family: A Consideration of Artificial Insemination by Donor*, London, 1981.

many children conceived through natural means are exposed to similar or comparable risks. But it is surely salutary to consider these dangers.

The first factor is one that might be expected to work to the child's advantage, but could quite conceivably act against it. While the conception of many children is planned by their parents, they are not deliberately and consciously brought into being in the way that artificially created children are. In a natural conception a child is the offshoot of an act in which two partners are interested principally in each other. Ironically, the fate of a child who has been so earnestly desired and deliberately fashioned may be that *too much* love and attention are focussed upon him or her. A child who falls short of expectations may then have a heavy burden to bear.

Secondly, the fact that the child has been *made* rather than been *begotten* may lead one to think of it less as a gift than a possession.[6] The child is the product of ingenious scientific manipulation of human gametes. Is it then liable to be thought of as an object which one has at one's disposal? This is probably less of a temptation for parents in relating to their artificially created children than for scientists deciding what to do with embryos in the laboratory. Because the scientists have 'made' the embryo, they appear to feel significantly more free to use it to further human knowledge than would be the case with embryos conceived through natural means.

Thirdly, the peculiarity of the artificially created child's origins expose it to the risk of being a person with obscure and insecure *roots*. Of course, the nature of its conception may be hidden from the child, but this brings its own perils in terms of the strain which keeping an intimate secret imposes on the couple concerned, and such deception is itself morally dubious. However, if the fact that a 'social' parent is not the 'natural' parent is revealed, this disclosure *is* likely to prove traumatic to the child. How deep the disturbance will prove to be depends on a whole range of psychological variables. The same sort of considerations also apply to adopted children, and for some the social acceptability of adoption and the apparent comparability of

---

6. The contrast between making and begetting children is well brought out by Oliver O'Donovan in *Begotten or Made?*, Oxford, 1984.

the family situations are sufficient to render objections to AID and other practices invalid. But there is a crucial difference: in the case of adoption the rootless child has already been created, and the act of adoption contains an element of response to the need of a child whose natural parents cannot give it the stable, loving environment which every child ought to have. Adoption involves the wrenching apart of a natural parental bond, but it happens when the prospects for the child are *nevertheless* thought to be better if this takes place. In the case of 'human assisted reproduction', to use Lady Warnock's phrase, a child with unusual (and possibly, in part at least, anonymous) genetic roots has been created deliberately. In a world where all too many children seem to suffer crises of identity through confusion about their origins, is it entirely responsible to add to their number?

These caveats, speculative as to some extent they are, do not constitute decisive grounds for rejecting the artificial aids to reproduction *en masse*. However, I believe that they are important considerations, which raise major questions about our society and our culture. The Warnock Committee was understandably wary about exploring them but also seriously negligent in failing to do so.

THE WARNOCK REPORT:
A VIEW FROM THE OTHER END

GEORGE L. CHALMERS

It may occur to some of you to wonder what a practising clinician in the field of Geriatric Medicine could possibly have to say about the report of the Committee of Inquiry into Human Fertilisation and Embryology. To be honest, it has occurred to me to wonder about precisely the same thing. The only valid contribution I feel able to make is that of a reasonably well-informed non-expert, with the advantage of medical education which allows me to know at least something of the context and also, usually, the meaning of the words.

First, let me state the obvious. The Warnock Report is not a Christian report, nor does it purport to be. It is a report by a group of distinguished people from the fields of education, law, obstetrics, general medical practice, neurology, psychiatry, midwifery, social work, theology and biology, whose backgrounds, opinions, feelings and values are as diverse as one might expect to find in any similar heterogeneous group. It is, however, a very full and comprehensive report and there are few issues in the field which it does not, at least, mention. This does not mean that its deficiencies, from a Christian point of view, are matters of positive difference, rather than the omission of important issues. It would be surprising, therefore, if we did not find areas, even major areas, of the Report which stand at variance with the Christian view of the ethics and morality of the subject.

Indeed, I had the clear impression that even the use of the term 'ethical', and of its near neighbour, 'moral', where they appear in the Report, was quite different from my own concept of them. I felt at times that the morality which I recognise as being a matter of right and wrong, was being replaced by a rather more nebulous concept regarding what is 'acceptable', and 'unacceptable', without too clear a notion of who it might be who was doing the accepting or otherwise. To the Christian, morality is quite clearly what is acceptable to God, and is related to the law and the values which we find in his revelation of himself in the Scriptures and, ultimately, in Christ.

The essence of this problem is suggested, perhaps, in the first paragraph of the Report. There is even at that stage a degree of confusion as to the use of the term 'ethical'. The Committee declare themselves reluctant to appear to dictate on matters of morals to the public at large. Yet, is not the public at large in need of guidance as to these very morals? I, in fact, had imagined that this was the principal reason for the setting up of this very body. The Committee, instead, 'sought for a steady and general point of view'. I am not sure that this is quite the same concept as an ethical or moral point of view in which the issues of what is *permissible*, rather than what is *acceptable*, are at stake.

We find, for example in para. 3, that some members had a clear perception of the family and its role within society, and in their consideration of the various techniques, their focus was upon the primacy of the interests of the child and on upholding family values. Others, however, 'felt equally strongly about the rights of the individual within society'. The implication is that these strong feelings on the part of the different members of the Committee, and, no doubt, on the part of those who gave evidence to it, required to be given equal weight, and that some sort of balance was necessary between them. Now morality, to the Christian, clearly indicates that the only valid context of reproductive activity is within the family structure and that the individual does not have reproductive rights in any other context. This is not a matter of consensus, it is a matter of right and wrong. It is wrong for the *individual*, wrong for the *child*, and wrong for *society*, to extend the bounds of this particular activity.

It seems to me, as a layman in such matters, that the Committee might have saved themselves whatever time was spent considering the 'rights' of single women, lesbians, single men and homosexuals, in the context of eligibility for treatment, had this simple principle of morality been applied. What 'right to treatment' for infertility does someone have who has not accepted a place in the normal structure of society for the procreation and up-bringing of children?

In 2.9 the Report states:

> Furthermore, the various techniques for assisted reproduction offer not only a remedy for infertility, but also offer the fertile single woman or lesbian couple the chance of parenthood without the involvement of a male partner.

I suggest that the techniques do nothing of the sort, it is those who manipulate them who may do so, and they are morally and ethically wrong so to do. The structure of marriage and the family - which is presumably what is defined as a 'loving, stable, heterosexual relationship' - is the right environment for the procreation of children. It has been since marriage was ordained, and I find no evidence that twentieth century man has found a better one. He may, perhaps, have proven his capacity to destabilise it, and this too is a major moral problem, but the family remains the normal and natural structure of society, and is, I believe, likely to continue so.

At this point my own professional interests are very much involved, since the support of the elderly depends very greatly upon the integrity and stability of family life, and many of the problems I meet are related to difficulties in this area. I do not wish to be overcritical about the choice of phrase in particular sections, but it seems incredibly lacking in conviction to state, as the Report does in section 2.11.

> We have considered these arguments, but, nevertheless, we believe that, as a general rule, it is better for children to be born into a two-parent family, with both father and mother, although we recognise that it is impossible to predict with any certainty how lasting such a relationship will be.

Have we really reached the level of pessimism about marriage at which we have to consider whether it is the best situation for the birth and raising of children? Would it not be fair to suggest that such an attitude of pessimism only helps to lower the expectations of stability in this most valuable, indeed precious of relationships?

It also seems strange that such a weak argument is proposed by a committee which equally argues that the treatment of infertility by some of the means under discussion will serve to cement and strengthen the family bond. I refer to section 4.14 in particular.

> It is not possible to predict future consequences of the growth of AID, but we would point out that those engaging in AID are, in their own view, involved in a positive affirmation of the value of the family.

And in 4.15: 'The fact that the couple share the experience of pregnancy in the same way as any other couple does, may strengthen their relationship as joint parents.' It is, of course, a matter of observation that the sharing of the experience of pregnancy may on occasion weaken rather than strengthen such a relationship, and this might apply with equal validity to any pregnancy. It was comforting to find an official body reaching the conclusion that the mere calculation of cost/benefit could not answer the question 'Is it right?', and one must concur that, in many areas, procedures and actions may be unacceptable whatever their long-term consequences are supposed to be.

Despite the wide diversity in feelings arising from religious, philosophical, or humanist beliefs, it became clear to the Committee that *people want some principles or other* to govern the use and development of new techniques. There is a recognised need for *some barriers* which are not to be crossed and *some limits fixed* beyond which people must not be allowed to go. The existence of morality is seen to depend upon it. Unfortunately, in the rest of the Report, the Committee seems remarkably reluctant to set such clear limits, and, when it does so, it is almost apologetic about it, setting them as wide as it feels it can. In their stated view (and few would argue with it?) a society without limits, especially in these areas, would be a society without moral scruples, and this nobody wants. But, is it true that nobody wants it? What need of a fence if nobody wishes to trespass? There does seem still to be some pressure for an even more permissive society than we currently experience.

I have spent rather a long time on the introductory section of the Report, but I think it is important to have done so, for it helps, perhaps, to clarify some of the other aspects over which Christian people may have difficulties with its terms, conclusions and recommendations. A great deal of significance lies, I believe, in these premises upon which the rest of the Report was based.

Infertility

There is, to my mind, no possible Christian objection to the use of all reasonable measures to relieve infertility within the bounds of the integrity of the family unit. We should, if we consider the several accounts of infertility in the Scriptures, hold a compassionate and constructive view of the desire for children which is usual and normal in any true marital bond, especially perhaps in Christian marriage. Such compassion will, naturally, support the Committee's desire to improve the very unsatisfactory state of the facilities for the assessment and treatment of infertility, so that proper premises, staffing and conditions are available for people seeking such help. It is reasonable for the infertile couple to seek assistance and for society to provide it properly.

AIH and possibly IVF may well have a place in such treatment, and this may be a matter for the conscience of the couple concerned, after full and careful counselling and discussion, rather than for total exclusion.

On the other hand, we have no licence to employ measures which threaten the sanctity of life, the sanctity of the marriage relationship, or the structure of the family or of society itself. In discussing AID, egg transfer and embryo donation, it is by no means clear that the undoubted intrusion of a third party, or even a fourth party, into the relationship of a couple will be as innocuous as their proponents would claim. It is not difficult to envisage the emotional rejection of such a child by one or other partner as 'Your child, but not mine' at some point of stress in the relationship, and even if this were not expressed, the presence of the child may well serve as a living reminder of inadequacy, in either partner, in an area of major personal and emotional importance.

The Warnock Report recognises these and other issues in setting out the argument, but is biased towards the use of these measures, possibly by the awareness that work is well advanced in these areas. It is interesting to note, in relation to surrogacy that, where it appears from Scripture to have been employed in patriarchal times, the initiatives came from man, rather than from God, and the action was an expression of the impatience of the individual concerned or of his wife or wives, rather than one motivated by faith. In each case also, the result was complication and difficulty for the family concerned, rather than a cementing of the family bonds. In these cases, of course, intercourse rather than artificial insemination took place with the surrogate, but the principle is the same. The Committee has, perhaps slightly reluctantly, recommended against surrogacy, but accepts the others as legitimate, despite the many difficulties which it clearly recognises, and hopes to relieve by alteration of legislation and by somewhat greater faith in the proposed licensing body than practical experience with similar bodies might support.

It is apparent that artificial insemination, and presumably AID, is regarded as a routine measure in some centres. We are given figures running into four figures for IVF from one clinic (para. 5.12), and surrogacy, in certain parts of the world, would appear to be a booming business already. This, undoubtedly, has made the task of the Committee much more difficult. It is one thing to recommend that an area of activity should not be permitted to develop, but quite another to recommend that it stop, or even that further study is necessary as to the ethical implications, before it is allowed to continue. It is very difficult to oppose a *fait accompli* and to dismantle a system which has become established, and it may be that, ideally, this body should have met several years ago when the techniques themselves were embryonic.

We cannot run the clock back to allow this, but I believe we ought not to allow what has been done to cloud the ethical issues, and we need to remind ourselves constantly that the mere fact that something can be done, or even has been done or is being done today, does not make it necessarily right, nor should it deter us from condemning it and seeking to stop it if it is wrong.

I believe that, as Christians, we may be guilty of obscuring the issues here ourselves. If a procedure has become established as a scientific fact, there is a tendency to accept that this is unchangeable, and therefore to rationalise it, rather than oppose it, perhaps because opposition is more difficult. We are capable of finding all sorts of reasons why it might be 'acceptable' in certain circumstances, and we then tend to extend the circumstances in exactly the same way as those who make less claim to ethical scruples. On the other hand, if something has not yet happened, we feel free to take a stand against it, on the grounds of moral or ethical principles.

Research

It is not difficult to justify embryo research, if our view of man is simply that he is a 'higher animal species', with no greater significance than any other. This, needless to say, is not the Christian view. A recognition of the unique elements of human personality, personhood and individual value are inherent in Christian commitment, as also is a concept of the spiritual nature of man, and, while it may be true that the proper study of mankind is man, this cannot be extended to the application of invasive experimentation.

This view, and its dilemma, are well stated in the Report at 11.14:

> Those who are firmly opposed to research upon human embryos recognise that a ban on their use may reduce the volume, not only of pure research, but also research in potentially beneficial areas, such as the detection and prevention of inherited disorders or the alleviation of infertility, and that in some areas such a ban would halt research completely. However, they argue that the moral principle outweighs any such possible benefits.

This statement does sound a little as if it is intended to make someone who holds this view feel bad about it, but it is a true dilemma, and it is right to state it, even if, in this instance, it may be a little overstated, as Professor Marshall and his co-dissenters point out in para. 6 of the expressions of dissent. If a principle is truly moral or ethical it stands above the pragmatic and the expedient, and, while the cost must be realised, it must also be faced if a true morality is to be conserved.

Doubtless many valuable lessons might have been learned from the experimental work carried out on human subjects in certain establishments in Nazi Germany, but the scientific community, rightly, rejected such work, whatever its scientific value, on moral and ethical grounds. Now, please do not misunderstand me. I am not equating current work with these other circumstances, I simply wish to underline the importance of setting ethical issues above expediency and pragmatism.

I was, frankly, relieved to read the terms of the minority report in the Expression of Dissent B of which Professor Marshall is a signatory. The case is clearly stated in the text, and has indeed been amplified elsewhere.

It seems to me that there are but two options when we consider when an embryo becomes a person. It is either at conception, or at birth. The period of time in between is a continuum of development, and it is eminently arguable that that continuum extends across the time of birth in such a way as to exclude any significant change in personhood being involved in the process of being born. To the Christian, the numerous references to prenatal experience, awareness and significance in the Bible should confirm the logic of such a view. The 14-day rule becomes unethical if we recognise the humanity of the embryo from conception, and irrelevant if we do not. If, indeed, there is doubt about this issue, is it not reasonable that the embryo, as the one least able to voice an opinion, should have the benefit of the doubt?

The idea of a variation in the value of a person related entirely to age is also worrying. If you are too young to matter at a certain point in life, however early, does there not come a time when you might also be too old to matter? Perhaps it is not too far from the care of the elderly after all, in practical ethical terms.

The concept of experimentation, or even of manipulation at this stage in life - the early embryonic - also causes me concern in respect of the potential for long term, unforeseen and unpredictable results. Several congenital abnormalities and familial diseases are not manifest until later life. Huntingdon's chorea springs readily to mind. If changes occur in the genetic material of the early developing cell, the margin of error is measurable in microns, and we have no way of knowing the effect of a tiny variation in the point at which DNA is split or re-combined, especially if that variation is extended over a period of a lifetime. We might well be setting the course for a human life with a defect in the compass which, while undetectable and apparently insignificant at the outset of the journey, may have much greater effects before its end. Some of us can recall that such an apparently innocuous environmental agent as oxygen administered inadvisedly, but with the best of intentions, to premature infants, resulted in many cases, in blindness due to retro-lental fibroplasia. As a geriatrician I am dealing with the later stages of life, and while the pre-natal problems of today will not affect me, I do have a real concern for my successors.

The whole area of human embryo research is fraught with so many imponderables that it may rival the research which brought us the nuclear age in its potential to damage the human race. It might be better, as well as morally right, to shut the lid of this Pandora's box before its contents blight the generations to come. Even if it does disturb the even tenor of the research laboratory, or reduce the publication list in someone's *curriculum vitae*, the need to protect what cannot be seen as other than human life is a fundamental principle, and cannot be replaced by a licensing body, no matter how strict and vigilant it may be.

The Report makes much of the 14-day rule as a safeguard against research which trespasses upon the rights of the unborn once they have gone beyond the 'clump of cells' stage. Frankly it seems to me that, even if it were ethically based, it is designed to be broken. The first stop will be the request for exception 'for sound scientific reasons' for a particular instance. This would reasonably be followed by the request for further exception 'for sound statistical reasons to corroborate previous work', and in due course the case for extension to 18, 21, or more days is progressively made and the ethical principle is steadily eroded. Unmentioned in this report is the subtle pressure of the researcher's personal involvement which is capable of blinding even the most meticulous when the issue at stake is a PhD thesis, or a good research record. Sometimes the researcher's conscience may require protection as well.

This element is hinted at in the Expression of Dissent at para. 8, where the 'strong temptation for doctors to harvest more embryos than are strictly required for the immediate therapeutic purpose in order to provide "spare" embryos' is mentioned. The generation of embryos for research is rejected as unethical. Why would this be different? Both would be excluded by the cessation of embryo research, and nothing in the Report or elsewhere convinces me that such research on human embryos is either necessary, justifiable or ethical. One cannot help feeling that once again the licensing body is being afforded excessive confidence as a means of control.

Future Developments

Chapter 12, dealing with Future Developments presents, to my mind, what is possibly the strongest case for bringing research to a halt. *Trans-species fertilisation* is apparently a reality, allowing men to prove their fertility by begetting a two cell hamster! It would seem that the fertilising power of the human sperm can be tested by fertilising a hamster ovum with it and then destroying it at the two cell stage (12.2). *Drug testing* is apparently an inviting field for the use of human embryos, and, while the pragmatic logic may seem unassailable, such a procedure would be wide open to exploitation on both scientific and commercial levels. One hears much of the protests of the 'animal rights' campaigners against the area of drug research on animals. Should we not see in this possibility - even if it is already a reality as it may well be - an even greater reason for protest?

Ectogenesis - the production of a human child in an entirely artificial environment - has the ring of science fiction, but may well be already more than the pipe-dream of a dedicated researcher somewhere. The purpose of such a project is suggested in para. 12.14 of the Report. 'This technique, it is argued, would make it possible to study in detail normal and abnormal human development at the embryonic and fetal stages.' Such babies would not, of course, belong to any emotionally involved father or mother, and the researcher could do what he wishes! Is this the way we wish to see research develop? The 14-day rule would stop it, but for how long?

Gestation in other species. The report says No! in clear terms, and deserves our fullest support.

Cloning, surely one of the ultimate arrogances of man, the production of another being in his own image, is not only possible, but even probable if current research continues, and I was disappointed to note that the Committee had no recommendations to make. They were, apparently, satisfied to note that it has been used successfully on other species, but, to the best of their knowledge, had not been carried out artificially on human embryos. If this be true, is not this the time to legislate to prevent it, rather than wait until it has?

Embryonic biopsy

Nucleus substitution - embryos for spare parts!

Prevention of genetic defects - genetic engineering.

The catalogue of arrogant interference seems endless. I have even heard the suggestion that scientists might be involved in 'engineering out effects of the fall!' but I suspect that they may be involved in nothing more dramatic than proving its reality. The opinion is apparently prevalent that 'there is no going back in research', and we find the attitude towards these issues expressed in the Report as 'pride in the new technology', allied with pleasure at the means to relieve the unhappiness of infertility. Pride is a dangerous entity in humankind, and it is such pride which generates most the 'unease at possibilities for manipulating the early stages of human development' which is mentioned at the same point in the Report.

The Committee constructed this Report taking into account the wide range of views in a pluralistic society and considering also the nature and value of clinical and scientific research, but declined to consider the possible impact of these issues upon the future of our society, on the grounds that it could not readily foresee what that impact might be. This seems reasonable, except that it is, none the less, quite prepared to support the continuance of research which has major potential to alter the shape of that future, by altering the values and structures upon which it stands.

Two applications of the research were perceived:
1. The benefit of the individual, and
2. The benefit of society as a whole by the pursuit of knowledge.

The Christian stands upon a totally different value structure, yet one which is capable of benefiting society to an even greater extent than technology has or ever will, and which bases its attitude to the individual on the principle of love. 'Inasmuch as ye did it unto the least of these . . . .' To quote Professor Torrance, 'The principle of loving objectively, for the other's sake, not for our own.'

The content of the Warnock Report casts my mind towards the account of the project of the tower of Babel, in which man's technology was overweening in its pride and no doubt was seen as being of the greatest potential benefit to mankind. It failed because it was contrary to the law and the purposes of God. Its whole ethos was contrary to the eternal law of love. That is, to the Christian, the ultimate touchstone of ethics and morality, and is applicable in this field as in all others.

INDEX

Abortion Act 1967, 93f, 100
Abraham, 78, 104
Adultery, 78
Archbishop of Canterbury, 77
Baptist Union of Scotland, 82, 86
Berry, R. J. 68
Brephos, 54
British Council of Churches, 90
British Medical Journal, 64
Brown, Louise, 74, 102
Cambridge Union Society, 39
Carriline, Madeline, 61f
Cartesian dualism, 64, 67ff
Cassuto, Umberto, 51
Catholic Bishops' Joint Committee on Bioethical Issues, 82, 84
Choices in Childlessness, 90
Church of England, General Synod of, 12
Church of England Board for Social Responsibility, 35, 59f, 82, 84, 86
Church of Scotland Board of Social Responsibility, 82ff, 88
Congregational Union, 82
David, 50
Ectogenesis, 76, 117
Edwards, Robert G., 26, 65, 102
Elizabeth, 54f
Embryo, Terms used for, 18f 58f
Ethics and Medicine, 5
Fall of man, 43f
Flood, Noachic, 43ff

Free Church Federal Council, 82, 90
Free Church of Scotland, 84, 86
Free Presbyterian Church of Scotland, 82, 85
General Medical Council, 81
Germany, Nazi, 41, 75, 114
Gormally, Luke, 73
Grisez, G., 72
Handbook of Medical Ethics, 28
Helsinki, Declaration of, 28, 30, 32, 40, 84
Helsinki Medical Group, 91
Higginson, Richard, 47
Holbrook, David, 64
Homo Sapiens, 6ff, 10, 19, 23
Houghton Committee, 97
Huxley, Sir Andrew, 67
Iglesias, Teresa, 33, 83
Image of God 10f, 13, 46f
Incarnation, 11ff
Infant Life Preservation Act 1929, 94
Jacob, 104
Jaki, Stanley, 55
Jakobovits, Sir I., 25
Jeremiah, 11, 50, 81, 74
Job, 50
John Paul II, 73
Jones, H., 65
Journal of Medical Ethics, 14, 25
Journal of the Christian Medical Fellowship, 51
Kant, Immanuel, 17, 41

Kuhse, Helga, 6ff, 13
Locke, John, 20
MacKay, Donald, 51ff
Mahoney, John, 68
Marshall, John, 61f, 87, 114
Mary, 12f, 54f
McCormick, Richard, 30f, 33
Mechanistic Darwinism, 64ff
Methodist Church Division of Social Responsibility, 82, 84, 86
Methodist Recorder, 87
Mitchell, D., 14f
Mitchell, G. D., 105
Monash University, 5f
New Scientist, 67
Norwich, Bishop of, 73
O'Donovan, Oliver, 5, 34, 106
Peel Committee, 93
Personhood, Idea of, 20ff
Polany, Michael, 60
Potentiality of the embryo, 8ff, 18, 32ff, 62
Powell, Rt Hon. Enoch, MP, 1
Purdy, J. M., 26, 65
Ramsey, Paul, 5, 29f
Royal College of General Practitioners, 82, 85, 90
Royal College of Nursing, 82, 85
Royal College of Obstetricians and Gynaecologists, 26f, 101
Rutherford House, 87

Scanlon, T., 20
Singer, Peter, 5ff, 13ff, 18f, 27
Slavery, 16f, 63
Snowden, R., 105
Society for the Protection of Unborn Children, 5
Soul, Idea of the, 56f, 69ff
Speciesism, 6ff, 10, 48
Steptoe, Patrick, 39, 102
Teichman, J., 22
The Times, 68, 100
Torrance, Thomas F., 9, 54, 84, 88, 118
Twinning and recombination, 69ff
Unborn Children (Protection) Bill, 1f
United Free Church of Scotland, 82
United Nations, 41
Utilitarianism, 15, 18, 40f
Virginal conception of Jesus, 54f
Von Rad, G., 45
Walker, Jean, 61
Walters, William, 7, 19
Weiser, A., 49
Wells, D., 14f, 18, 27
Westermann, C., 46
Winston, Robert, 37
Wittgenstein, 22
Woollam, David, 91
World Health Organisation, 84
World Medical Association, 28, 101